THE CRAFT AND CREATION OF WOOD SCULPTURE

CECIL C. CARSTENSON

edited by
WILLIAM S. BROWN

DOVER PUBLICATIONS, INC. NEW YORK

Published in Canada by General Publishing Company, Ltd., 30 Lesmill Road, Don Mills, Toronto, Ontario.
Published in the United Kingdom by Constable and Company, Ltd., 10 Orange Street, London WC2H 7EG.

This Dover edition, first published in 1981, is an unabridged republication of the work originally published by Charles Scribner's Sons, New York, in 1971. A newly revised list of suppliers has been included in this Dover edition.

International Standard Book Number: 0-486-24094-0
Library of Congress Catalog Card Number: 80-68448

Manufactured in the United States of America
Dover Publications, Inc.
180 Varick Street
New York, N.Y. 10014

AUTHOR'S PREFACE

There is a need for a book of this sort. In this day of increased leisure time, increased educational participation and increased interest in the arts there is a dearth of good instructional texts on direct carving, particularly in wood. I honestly feel that the practice of wood sculpture would be more pervasive if there was more knowledge available about the art. The book tries to fill that need.

We are talking directly to the beginner here, the student or hobbyist who brings no knowledge of the subject with him. For this reason I hope the art teachers using this text will have patience with its didactic flavor. I am only trying to make sure that the beginner who cannot rely on a teacher's guidance will get the point. My intentions are described by Montaigne: "All I say is by way of discourse, and nothing by way of advice. I should not speak so boldly if it were my due to be believed."

This book would not have come to life without the good efforts of William Brown. I thank him for fitting my words onto these pages. I also am indebted to Myron Wold for defining his beautiful Hawaiian woods, and to George Longfellow for his manuscript advice. My greatest gratitude, of course, goes to all of those who have made the world of sculpturing so satisfying and continually fascinating. Not least of these would be my wife, Blanche.

There is a need for a book of this sort. I hope you find that this particular one fills that need.

EDITOR'S NOTE

During the Fall of 1967 I taped about thirty hours of conversation with the artist at work in his workshop. He discussed all phases of his art, as well as other entertaining subjects that do not belong in this book. He is always interesting and it was difficult to remove any of it from the text.

Because of this aural method of gathering information and because of Mr. Carstenson's lucid way of discussing any topic, I have used a more conversational tone than is found in most texts. I hope you do not find this annoying. His message seems more alive when it is "spoken" rather than falsely rendered into textbook English. The cliches and anecdotes are meant not to cloy, but to underscore the pure enjoyment of sculpturing.

A word about the pictures: of the 77 sculptural pictures, two-thirds of them are work-in-progress, necessarily the author's own. The remaining pictures are his own work also, chosen to indicate the range of any artist's repertoire. Their selection is meant to be one of instruction and not one of egocentricity. Our job is to show the student what is possible, to explain why a certain form was chosen, and to relate how a design change developed during the execution of a piece. Only work with which the artist has been personally involved allows him this capability. The art histories are filled with famous and familiar works of art which the student is encouraged to study. The instructional advice of a living American artist seems more helpful in a text of this sort than yet another picture of "Winged Victory." That is the only reason for not including others' works here.

My role is one of organization and editing. If, in the process of this task, I have paraphrased incorrectly or omitted pertinent information, thus misstating the author's meaning, the mistake is mine for which I apologize and accept all responsibility.

CONTENTS

THE CRAFT AND CREATION OF WOOD SCULPTURE

ONE

TOOLS

THE WORKSHOP

BEFORE you do anything you need a place to do it. If you feel that the type of place is not so important, that you can work anywhere, then you are absolutely right. Unfortunately not everyone is as enlightened as you. The saddest alibi of all is the one that goes, "Well, I just don't have a place to work." These words are the most obvious sign of a dilettante. When he refers to a place to work it is never a workshop, always a studio. I personally don't care for the word "studio" because it conjures up images of witty people sitting about with teacups in their hands discussing literature. I discuss literature in my shop, too, but I can't get a lot of sculpturing done with a teacup in my hand. You don't need a place to entertain. You need a place to cut wood.

I started out in a corner of my bedroom. I worked there for years, and some of those pieces now reside in museums. The place was adequate for my needs. I had very few tools at the time and really no other place to set up. Except for a few stray woodchips in the bedsheets that riled my wife a bit, that "studio" was fine for what I wanted to accomplish. That is why I become distraught when I hear some of my acquaintances say they just don't have a suitable place to work. I visit their houses and find beautiful two- and three-car garages sitting half empty, and that is before I even get inside.

It is important when you are looking for a place to put your things, and you really do need a place to put them, to think of it as a workshop and not as an artist's studio. Then your choice won't be artificially limited.

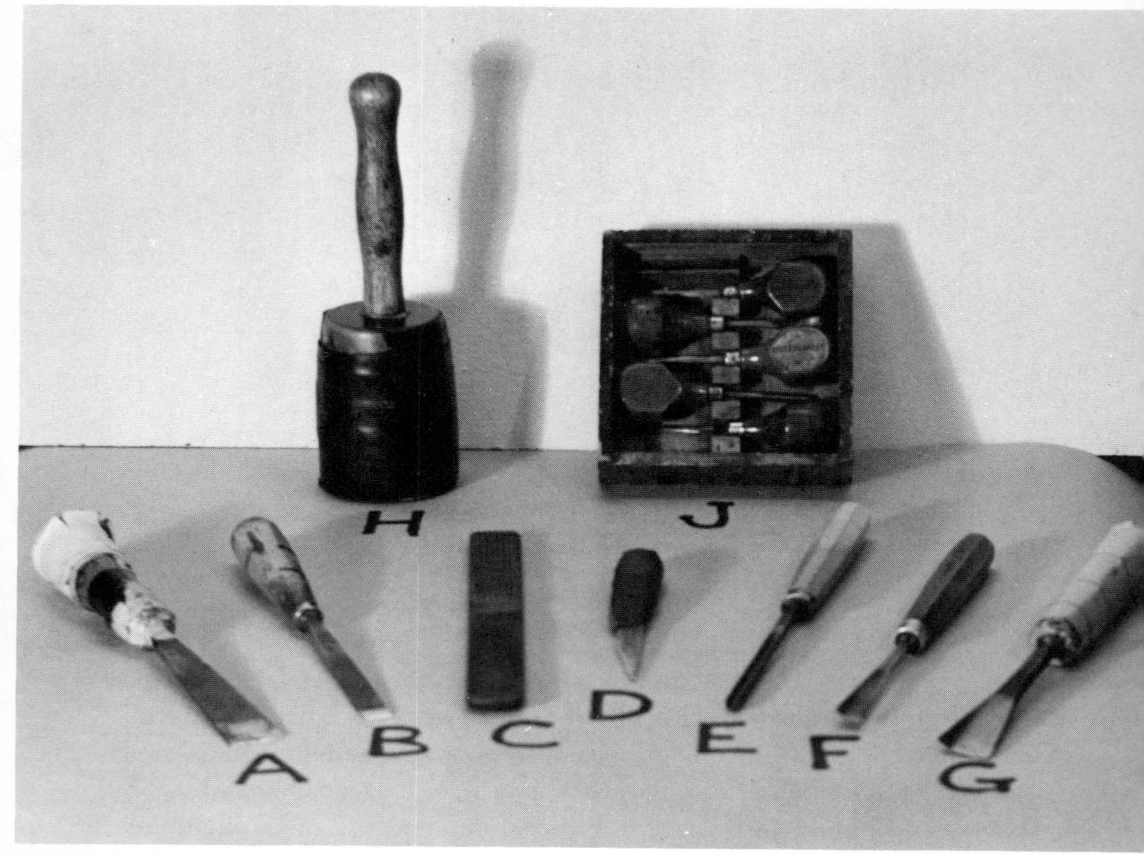

Fig. 1. The basic tools: (A) one-inch chisel; (B) half-inch chisel; (C) rasp; (D) knife; (E) deep gouge; (F) half-inch #5 gouge; (G) one-inch #5 gouge; (H) mallet; (J) linoleum cutting set. For years these were all the tools I owned.

If you work hard and become famous you can have your "studio" anywhere and anyhow you want it. My present shop is in my basement and I consider it just fine for my purposes. You can even drink tea there if you wish.

BASIC TOOLS

Investment in tools and equipment can run anywhere from the bare essentials for $25*(Fig. 1) to a professional's investment of several thousand dollars. If you are just starting out, you definitely will want to restrict yourself to a minimum number of tools until you find out whether you really like to sculpt.

*Prices quoted were accurate in 1971. Allowances should be made for subsequent inflation.

BUY THE BEST

Always buy the best tools you can find. An inexpensive tool will let you down by not holding its edge. This causes two problems. It will wear out or break quickly, leading to excessive sharpening and rapid junking. If you continue in your craft you will end up spending much more to replenish your worn-out kit than if you had bought high quality equipment to begin with. Even more crucially, if the neophyte begins with poor equipment and it performs poorly, it may unduly discourage him from pursuing the art.

Tools are expensive and continue to become even more expensive each year. Get a good grip on your pocketbook and buy a few of the best items you can find, rather than spending all your budget on inferior brands that will soon be worthless.

USE YOUR OWN

Always use your own tools. If you teach, please do not put together a departmental kit to be passed out indiscriminately to one and all. If you must have school-owned equipment, buy enough to check out a basic kit to each student at the beginning of the course to be returned at the end. The reasons for this are obvious. A person will take care of his own tools, handle them properly, store them properly, sharpen them properly and not lose them. Take pride in your tools. In a very real sense your work can only be as professional as the condition of your tools. When you hear people bemoaning the lack of craftsmen any more, remember that the old tradesman kept a boxful of impeccably cared for equipment. The respect he gave his tools shone through in his work.

The basic kit (Fig. 1) consists of five cutting edges, a rasp and a mallet. These seven items, plus some sort of holding device, can be purchased for about $25. A few suppliers are listed in the Appendix.

Chisels and Gouges: Get a #5 or #6 one-inch and #5 or #6 half-inch gouge. The number describes the radius, or curvature, of the cutting edge, spanning from 1, which is flat, to 12 or so. There are other numbering schemes, varying with suppliers, but this is the standard one. The inch and half-inch refer to the distance between cutting edge points. You will also want a half-inch deep gouge, somewhere around a number 8, 9 or 10.

The only difference between a chisel and a gouge is that the cutting edge of a chisel is flat. The cutting edge is not curved. Be sure to get a craftsman's chisel which is V-shaped on the end allowing you to cut either way, rather than the familiar carpenter's chisel which is flat on one side and beveled on the other. This will not work well in sculpturing. You will want to buy a number 1 one-inch and half-inch chisel.

These five tools will allow you to handle most cutting problems that arise. A good tool will cost about $3. I can recall them being 68 cents, but the price of tools belies the old saying that what goes up must come down. Tool prices just keep going up. By the way, cutting tools come from the supplier dull, so be sure to sharpen them before use, as is explained in Chapter Three.

Mallet: You will need a mallet to hit these chisels and gouges with. As with other tools, get a good grade carving mallet of lignum vitae or hickory. An important consideration here is the size of the mallet. If you are young and masculine you will think that you should get a big one. The typical healthy nineteen-year-old makes the mistake of thinking that sculpture is a violent battle of brawn and he gets a big heavy mallet. He is wrong on at least two counts. The tool edges will not hold up under that constant big bang. Neither will his arm. You should conserve energy, no matter how young and virile you assume yourself to be. If you become serious about sculpturing you are going to be raising and lowering that mallet hundreds of thousands of times. Be smart and get a moderate-sized one. Mallets cost from two to three dollars.

I wrap my mallets with rubber tape. Atfer years and years of listening to the sharp rapping of mallet against chisel handle I began to develop what is referred to as "boilermaker's ear." It affected my hearing. This worried me, and I wrapped tape around my mallets hoping to deaden the sound. It works beautifully. It also extends the life of my mallets indefinitely. I have never worn one out since wrapping them, and that has been more than ten years. I also wrap my chisel and gouge handles in ordinary masking tape. If I don't, I find myself changing handles after eight or ten hours of tool usage. The constant pounding causes them to fray and split. I now lose handles after eight or ten years. The minute that it takes to wrap the handles is worth it.

Rasp: You are probably familiar with rasps or files and what they can do. Buy the best quality rasp that you can find. A 10- or 12-inch normal half-round rasp will suit your purposes. A half-round is convex on one side and flat on the other. We will discuss rasps at greater length when you are doing your first piece. A good rasp costs about two dollars.

Holding Device: Learn this basic, most important truth. To produce decent sculpture you will need a holding device. If your material isn't pinned down it slides, bounces, jostles and generally does not behave the way that it should. Later on we will talk about how you must maintain constant physical control of your medium. Without a holding device this is impossible.

If you can, buy a good woodworker's vise right now (Fig. 2, Item V). Get a good quality bench vise with a stationary and movable jaw operated by a rotating arm. A Columbian or Wilton vise is good and costs about $25. If you just can't spend that much right now there are some cheaper alterna-

Fig. 2. Here are some holding devices. The (A)'s are both power arms, one with work mounted on it; (B)'s are various blocks used to mate the material to the holder; (C1) is a home-made clamp, a variation of (C3); (C2) is a familiar C-clamp; (C4)'s are furniture clamps; (V) is a woodworker's vise; (W) represents various wedges; (X)'s are vise pads that buffer the wood from the vise jaws.

tives. Fasten a short length of two-by-four to your workbench. Bolt a similar block close to one end of the first one. You now have a wedge. Prop your material inside this wedge and fasten the movable end with a dowel through a hole in the bench or with a C-clamp. This is the world's cheapest holding device, aside from your lap—which won't do. It will suffice until you have explored sculpturing a little more.

SUMMARY

These tools, along with a linoleum cutting set and a good knife, pictured in Fig. 1, were all that I used for years. The only disadvantage in not having a more elaborate array of tools was a loss of efficiency. This is all you need to get started. I once knew a rich young man who became inspired with the idea of sculpturing. He asked me what tools he needed to do professional work. Foolishly, I told him. He bought everything, and after three half-done pieces he realized that his inspiration had waned. I felt awful. If you buy the basics and become disenchanted you can always resell them at a decent price. Don't make me feel awful again.

Rather than cluttering up your mind with a lot of information about other tools that you may wish to buy later on, why don't you go on to the beginning of the next chapter now. After you have completed a piece or two you can come back and learn more.

MORE ABOUT TOOLS

Now that you are somewhat familiar with the handling of the basic tools, it is time to discuss others.

HOLDING DEVICES

Experience has already taught you the utter necessity of keeping your material firmly in place. You need a holding device. There are two types: vises and wedges (Fig. 2). It matters not what you use as long as the material is solid. A vise closes down upon the wood, while a wedge is relatively immovable and the material is jammed into its narrowing walls.

I have used a number of holders over the years, ranging from the two-by-four arrangement described earlier to elaborate homemade and commercial devices. The important thing is to have something that will hold the work solidly.

For years I used modified furniture clamps (Fig. 2, Item C4). They work well but don't have the flexibility of other devices. Any catalog house, such as Sears or Wards, carries them. I modified mine to cradle the wood more easily.

Sooner or later you have got to decide whether you like this business or not. Assuming that you do, let me suggest that you screw up your courage and buy a good woodworker's vise. It will cost about $25, your first big outlay, but it will be worth it. Think of it as three or four nights' bowling. You will certainly derive more pleasure from it than a few hours of diversion would give. These vises are heavy and should be mounted on a good strong workbench. One poor student proudly bought a big vise and nailed it down to a wobbly old end table. He couldn't understand why the vise didn't improve his work. It wiggled when you looked at it. Locate a strong bench. With all the working of the material, laterally as well as vertically, the joints will have to be solid. It shouldn't give when you lean against it. Bolt, do not nail, your vise to the bench. There is so much natural give in wood itself that you don't need to compound the problem with a shaky base.

I use a power arm most of the time now (Fig. 2, Item A). It costs about the same as a good vise. The beauty of a power arm is in its flexibility. You can turn it to any angle that you wish and lock it into place. If your enthusiasm is genuine this is the holder to own, along with the standard woodworker's vise.

The power arm is a simple swivel and lock, based on a ball joint similar to your hip socket. There is a flat platform atop this swivel to which you attach wooden mounting blocks (Fig. 2, Items B, B1 and B2) or sometimes the piece itself. These blocks are to adapt the base of the piece to the power arm, and also to allow full use of the material. I use elm for my mounting blocks because it is extremely tough. They last for years.

The blocks are prepared by drilling several holes slightly larger than the diameter of the holding screws. This allows the screws to be easily inserted through the block. Drill correspondingly smaller holes that approximate the inside diameter of the threaded portion of the screw into the piece itself. If these holes are too small the wood will split; if they are too large the screw will strip out the wood. Experience will help you here. Use several screws to hold the piece to the block securely. Hard woods may re-

Fig. 3. Another look at some holders. Sculpturing material (S) sits in the vise, the cradle, and in a clamp on the power arm. The dowel board in back is handy for holding oddly shaped pieces. The dowels are movable. The old ironing board on the right is my portable tool shelf.

quire lag bolts with lockwashers and washers between the bolt head and the block to create the holding tension, rather than relying on the screw threads. The screws need not penetrate the wood more than one-half to one inch to hold it rigidly. Be sure to mark on the base of the wood the depth of the screws (Fig. 18). The block is then fastened to the platform with either lag bolts or screws at each corner.

Always keep the holder, no matter which type, fastened snugly. Turn your work at an angle that will allow the mallet to drive the material into the holder, rather than loosening it. If you use a vise, keep several padded blocks around that are wrapped with paper. These are excellent for protecting your piece while you are finishing up.

The funny-looking object at the right in Fig. 3 is invaluable. It is a cockeyed sawhorse. It is important that you build it askew with no straight or parallel lines. It is uncanny how you can plunk any thick or unwieldy piece into that cradle and have it sit as snugly as in a giant vise. I couldn't get by without this item.

There is an infinite number of devices. Use your ingenuity and you can come up with just the right holder for a particular problem. I can't show all my ideas here, and indeed it is better that you devise your own. Any good sculptor soon learns to develop his own bag of tricks. For example, I have had trouble finding just the chisel I wanted when I wanted it. I found that an old ironing board my wife was throwing out was a perfect portable tool holder on which I could lay out my tools. If I didn't have it I would have been forced to invent it.

Don't be afraid to use your ingenuity in developing ways to hold your work. It must be solid and it should be open to your tools. If you can afford it, get a woodworker's vise or a power arm—or both. If you can't right now, that is perfectly all right. You are only missing mobility. If you think that you will be able to afford one in a few months, however, go out and get it now. You won't regret it.

SCRAPERS AND SLICERS

As the ability and desire to increase the tool kit grows, considerable interest will arise in the ways of scraping and slicing the excess wood away from your idea.

Rasps and Files: Fig. 4 shows the difference between rasps and files. A rasp tears away the wood with individual teeth whereas a file wears away the material with intersecting knife edges. Rasps are relatively faster,

Fig. 4. The left sketch shows the independent teeth of a rasp, while the right one depicts the crosshatchings of a file.

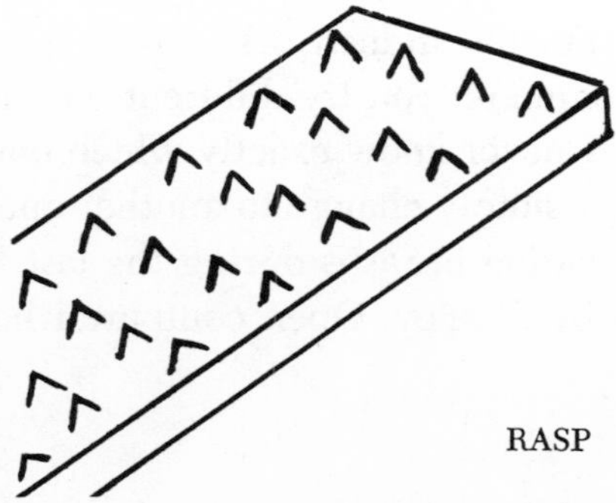

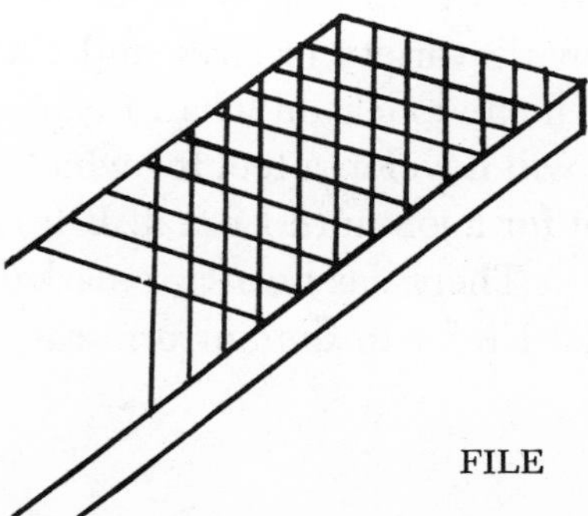

but because of the individual tearing action they leave deeper grooves than files.

The similarity, of course, is in their general appearance and usage. They come in all shapes, sizes and weights, and each one is different. I have hundreds of rasps and files. As you progress you will find yourself leaning first on one, then another. The most important thing to learn, as with all tools, is to get the best quality rasps and files that you possibly can. There is no economizing in this category. Some suppliers are suggested in the Appendix. Once you adopt a favorite tool and gradually wear it out you will find it hard to replace. There are no large manufacturers of craftsman's tools. You must buy through a sculptor supply catalog house and do a lot of comparative shopping.

Sizes are at once simple and misleading. They are simple in length: inches in the U.S. and centimeters in other countries; simple in cutting size: regular (usually marked with an "R" or unmarked) and smooth (marked "S"). This refers to the height of the cutting burrs. They are misleading as there is no industrial standard, and one firm's smooth will be another's regular. Trial and error is king in the land of rasps and files. Shop around and find a particular supplier that you like and stay with him. American tools are superior but limited in size and shape. Some foreign countries make better tools than others. I recommend German, Swiss, English, and some Italian tools.

Most of you are familiar with the many varieties and types: round or rat-tail rasps, mill and bastard files. The mill file's grooves, for example, cut straight across and are smoother than the bastard file, whose grooves are cut at an angle. The bastard file is better for soft woods. The important thing is to have both curved and flat files for the various tasks that will arise. You can get by with just the basic horseshoe rasp, but adding more will ease your job and save you time. I even keep old worn files for cleaning up other files' teeth marks.

These tools are used to clarify forms in progress, and to remove wood slowly in touchy spots. As these tools respond differently because of the wide variety of sizes and classes within the industry, I cannot specify which one to use on what. I can only recommend you try different ones and you will develop a feel for which is best. I never know exactly which one is right for a job until I use it. If it is wrong I simply change to another one.

There has been a remarkable innovation in rasps during the last few years. I refer to the Surform rasps made by Stanley. Open contoured holes replace the conventional teeth, acting like a kitchen shredder. They come in various shapes and sizes and I am sold on them until something better comes along. The work goes so much faster without being torn to pieces.

Riffles: As you become more affluent you will definitely want to get a few riffle rasps (Figs. 21 and 36). You can get along without them but they are very helpful to have around. These are small curved rasps of varied design. They are sold by overall length. I had only a few for years, but they insidiously became a passion. I have accumulated over four boxes of them, each one unique. They cost from about $1.75 to $2.00 each. They are especially good for the detailed work at the end of a piece. It doesn't matter what shapes you get just so they differ. Again, you will have to cultivate your supplier as quality varies enormously.

Scrapers: A scraper is invaluable. It is not a standard commercial tool although there are inferior scrapers on the market; inferior because they are too flimsy, being only .012 inches thick. It is relatively easy to make one, however. Obtain strips of any good Swedish or American spring steel—stock used for door-springs—at any specialty hardware store. Get a thickness of .025 inches and about 3/4 of an inch wide. It is a tough metal and you will have to put it in a vise and bend it back and forth to break it. Use a grindstone or a handfile and shape it into any shape you might want to get into a tight spot. The cost of the material is negligible, the nuisance of getting and shaping the steel being the only problem. Banding material or hacksaw blades will not work properly. Glass works, but you can never find the right shape, it is dangerous to use, and it is coarser than spring steel. After you have the shape you want run the grindstone or file straight against it to make a burred edge. This cutting edge is better than sandpaper, which is inefficient, slow and hard to control, particularly on hard woods.

Knives: There is seldom a piece that doesn't require a knife someplace. A knife can get into places that other tools cannot approach. It is neither efficient nor safe, but it works. Get a good knife. A boy scout knife is not sturdy enough. X-Acto knives aren't strong enough either. Most pocketknives are worthless. The best craftsman's knife I have owned is fashioned from a shirt knife (Fig. 1, Item D). It is the best blade that can be found, used in tailor shops for cutting out thick layers of cloth for shirts. I have had only two all my life. A blade costs 35 cents. As you can see in Fig. 1, I fashioned a simple wooden handle around the blade and wrapped it with layers of friction tape. All you buy is the blade.

AIDS AND INGENUITY

Why More? I keep saying that I got along for years with just five chisels, a mallet and a couple of rasps and did professional work, and yet I also keep saying that you should go out and get some more tools whenever you can. I'm not confused. It is a matter of economics. Additional tools save you time and energy. I wasted a lot of time because I didn't have the tool that would do the job the easiest. I simply felt I could not afford the tool so I did the job the hard way. If a person is going to stay with sculpture, then he should buy as many tools as he can to become more efficient. If I had had sense and guidance enough in the early days to buy fifty tools, I would be so much further along; but I had neither.

I don't want to misguide you on the cost of equipment. Yes, you can set yourself up a minimum kit for $25 or so. As you become more immersed in the craft, however, the investment mushrooms. A conservative estimate of my physical plant, which is relatively complete and well-stocked, would list:

Hand tools	over $1500
Bench fixtures	600
Power tools	500
Wood and supplies	6000
Minimum total	$8600

These figures may scare you. They scare me. Yet I know several well-off men who just hate to spend money on a tool. They will go out for dinner with their wives and eat a dozen tools at one sitting.

I use about 75 tools on an average piece, and I know that I use that many because when I clean up I put that many away. This only means that when you do things from a commercial standpoint you find the best and easiest tool to do the job. This is important. To put it simply, the advantage of having lots of tools is that you can reach for the one that is the right size and shape to do a specific task efficiently.

If you really want to do sculpture, buy tools. You should do the buying yourself. Only you know what tool you need. Buy it only when you need it. When you find that you can't really do a particular job properly—that you need a smaller or larger tool—that is when you need it and that is when you should buy it. You should not necessarily have the same tools that I have. You should not have the same tools that Henry

Moore has. We each do our work differently. Drop hints to your wife or to your friends around the holidays or your birthday about the splendid little tool that is all you would need to become really expert. It works.

Auxiliary Tools: I made an important self-discovery while working on this book. I have conjured up and whomped together more tools over the years than I have bought. At one time or another I was faced with a special situation and the need for just such a special device—one that I didn't have and couldn't buy—so I invented it myself. There are lots of commercial aids that I have used, but the important thing to remember is that there comes a time when your own ingenuity is the only thing that can get you out of a certain jam.

Some commercial tools are helpful. A veiner, for example, is a V-shaped gouge that can cut deep grooves with and against the grain. Don't buy one right away. It is more important to become used to handling the other chisels and gouges first. The reason that many people have trouble with this little tool is that they haven't learned one secret: a veiner cuts cross-grain and if one is careless the wood is going to tear. It is also difficult to control the depth of the trough. Once you learn to control the veiner you can cut a line with it in any direction. It is very useful for outlining your work in progress. It gives you a relatively non-destructive preview of how the piece will look later on.

Burring tools are in all the craftsman catalogs, but don't be in too big a hurry to buy them. They are small electric drills with tiny burrs, or toothed balls, that tear out little grooves of wood. Frankly, I find that the small ones aren't powerful enough to do much good and the big ones cost too much. I use them to texture some hardwood pieces and to hollow out hard-to-reach places. Someone gave me a set and I bought a commercial grinder for about $30. This increased their utility, but they would never be number one on my shopping list. As you can see in Fig. 5, tools proliferate. I think they breed at night. If a person is going to make this a serious hobby—or more—he has got to be prepared to do anything to accomplish his goals. He needs the tools to do it. Let me name a few that I use constantly:

Socket wrenches (to fasten bolts to bases)
Various scrapers and spoke shavers
Scriber
Ruler

Fig. 5. Typical auxiliary tools.

Curved rasps (good for open surfaces)
Hand drills
Knives of all kinds
Card files and brass brushes
Calipers (really useful—I don't use them much any more but I had them in my hands half the time when I was beginning. Models hate them, especially on cold days.)
Common tools (saws, hammers, planes and screwdrivers)
Brushes (sashbrush, toothbrush, shaving brush)
Magnifying glass (to check tool tips)
Safety glasses and dust masks
Block and tackle (for lifting and moving heavy pieces of material)

POWER TOOLS

The beginner's first craving is for power tools. With easy nonchalance he gobbles the rules of basic tool technique only to discover them hard to digest. He gets so exasperated that he just wants to get the darn thing over with in a hurry. That is one thing that power tools will do: get it over with in a hurry.

People think that a handpainted picture is inherently good. Big deal. If it were footpainted it would be just as valid, if the artist had a good foot. It is difficult to paint well by foot, though, or by hand for that matter. The fine sculptor Jacques Lipchitz was once asked by a little girl, "Mr. Lipchitz, is it hard work to make a good piece of sculpture?" He answered, "Yes, and also it is hard work to make a bad one." The point is that if power tools help your idea along don't be ashamed to use them. There is nothing intrinsically wrong with using power tools. A steam shovel would be legal if it worked. The problem lies in letting the tool come between you and your idea. It can do this in two ways.

With a few exceptions, nature abhors a straight line. Machines love straight lines. A piece of sculpture should have a million silhouettes. The machine won't let you have them. There has been some serious work done by bandsaw—there is even a book out on it—but every piece created in this manner looks like a cut-out. The piece gets caught in the lines of the machine.

The other problem is speed. Power tools can take off wood faster than you can think. You have got to have stalling time when sculpturing so that you can puzzle out the problems. I find myself getting a cup of coffee when I don't really want one, just so I can stop and ponder on the problems of the piece I am working on. I am stalling although I am usually not conscious of it. With power tools you don't stall. You just cut wood.

I do use several power tools with caution. Electric drills can be used to put a hole where you definitely know you will need a hole. The problem, of course, is to *know* how you are going to use the hole. Usually you don't know until you are further along.

Circle saws, or bench saws, are constructive when you must prepare bases or make small pieces from large, but I can think of no creative way in which to use a circle saw.

A bandsaw, or jigsaw, can be used when you definitely want to take off a section that you know has to come off. The key word again is *know*. It is so seldom that we actually do know. Once you know, however, there is no reason in the world that you can't use a bandsaw. The more you learn the more you can use a power saw. I personally don't dare go within a half-inch of my line or I might commit myself before I should.

Power grinders (Fig. 6) are a real asset for sharpening tools and you should get one as soon as you can. They save a lot of time and they do a better job.

Remember, there is no merit in doing it by hand if you can do it as well with a power tool. They are fine if you know what you are doing, but you have to know a lot more than I do before you can be at your ease with them. If I had been trained to use pneumatic chisels and power saws when I began I might be more comfortable with them, but I am inclined in my prejudice to think not. As it is, I can work for ten hours at a stretch without power tools, so I don't miss them too badly.

TOOL CARE

Sharpening: There are all sorts of sharpening devices. Between the homemade strop and the power grinder is the well-known honing stone, described in Chapter Three. You can sharpen better and faster with an electric grindstone. You can't sharpen rasps, of course, but your chisels and gouges will last for years with proper care.

Buy a good grinding machine, with a grindstone on one end of the shaft and a felt wheel for intermediate sharpening on the other. Grind-

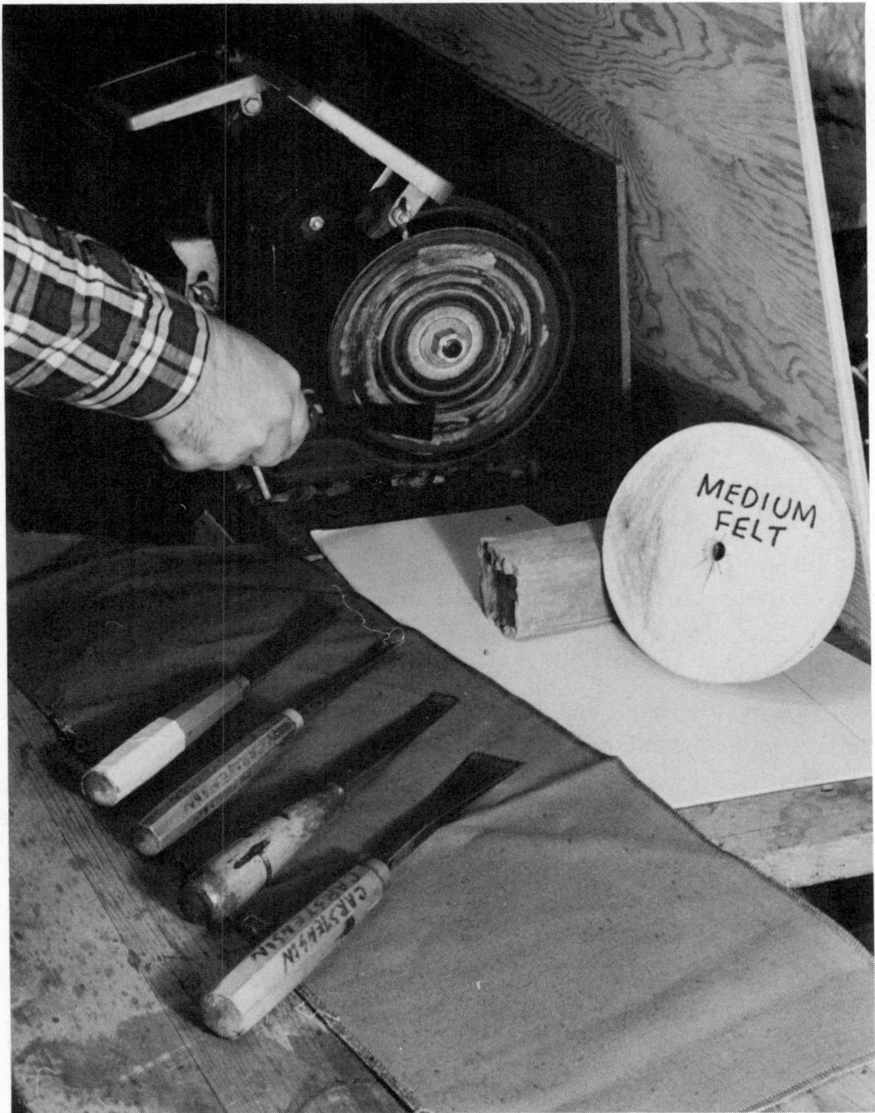

Fig. 6. Honing a gouge on the side of a felt wheel. A spare wheel is leaning against a bar of S2 Compound which has already been applied to the wheel. Rock the edge back and forth for uniform honing.

ing wheels come in different weights. Get the heavy-duty standard grade. Felt wheels can be obtained from the supplier. A medium felt wheel is what you want. Use it to hone gouges by applying a generous amount of S2 stainless steel compound bar on the side of the wheel while it is at rest. This compound contains fine particles of abrasive material which attack the surface of the tool steel applied against it. Putting the compound on while the wheel is turning will send bits of S2 stainless steel compound bar all over the room. Figs. 6 and 7 illustrate the use of the wheel. The wheel is rotating counterclockwise so the tools are held on the downward portion of the wheel. The tool edge should drag with the motion. To go against it would destroy either the wheel or the tool. Fig. 6 shows how the gouge is held against the side of the wheel. Fig. 7 shows that chisels can be honed on the edge. A gouge held there would result in an uneven edge. Remember always to be careful around a grinder.

An important reason for buying more tools is that different woods require different cutting edges. To make it simple, soft wood requires razor-sharp edges for clean cuts. A blunt edge would merely bull its way through the loose fibers. Conversely, a razor-sharp edge against oak or ebony would simply break off. Hard wood needs blunter tools. I have three sets of tools. One is for basswood and soft pine and it has razor-sharp edges. One is for medium woods such as walnut. Its edges are more bullet-shaped so that the shock of contact can be distributed more evenly over the mass of the tool. For hard wood I use a third set, even more bulbous. Thin edges don't last long with rosewood or lignum vitae. Blunt tools on softer wood will mar and tear rather than cut. These multiple sets of tools will save the hours of sharpening and resharpening and eventual destruction demanded of only one set.

Old files can be sharpened on a grindstone to have perfectly square ends. These act as excellent scrapers, especially on hard woods. The depth of cut depends upon the height of the worn teeth and the width of the file. They can get into spots that other tools just will not reach.

Repair: Learn how to repair broken tools. Sometimes a flaw in the metal will allow a crack to form which will eventually cause a break. Examine the broken area closely. If the metal is not clear and bright, if it is dull-colored, then it is flawed. Chipped edges of more than a fraction of an inch would take forever to repair on a felt wheel or by hand. Use the grinder. Draw a line on the tool that evens out the cutting edge. Dip the tool end in water and then apply it to the grinder for a few seconds. Dip it in the water again and repeat. Continue until the desired line is reached. The water is very important as it retains the temper, or strength, of the steel. If a tool loses its temper it will become soft and fail to stand

Fig. 7. A flat chisel can be honed by being held against the circumference of the wheel. Hold it firmly. The grindstone is on the other end of the shaft.

up under cutting pressure. If it becomes too hot the temper will make the tool brittle and it will break off again. If necessary, a tool can be re-tempered by heating the working edge to a cherry red and then plunging it into the coldest liquid you can find. This will restore its life.

Once you have cut back past the flaw line, slowly rotate the gouge against the side of the grindstone until a contoured edge is formed. Continue to keep the edge relatively cool. Also try to keep the cutting edge symmetrical. Now make the edge blunt for hardwood or sharp for softwood. Examine the edge with a magnifying glass and decide whether it is properly formed. If so, sharpen it on the felt wheel. If you have no power grinder, I personally think you would be wise to go to a carpenter's shop and have it repaired in a few minutes for a dollar or less. This operation is nothing but drudgery by hand.

Safety: Always know where the other hand is. If your tools are in proper condition they are sharp. One could slice through a hand very easily and very quickly. You must be cognizant of the potential danger all the time, at every moment.

Every sculptor must be aware of the potential danger of tetanus in all wood. The dirt found in any wood is a splendid breeding ground for tetanus germs. When you work with wood, particularly hardwood, you are going to nick your skin occasionally and allow these germs to enter your system. Keep your tetanus shots current every five years or so.

I wear a dust mask when doing heavy sanding. I also wear safety glasses when working around the grinder or even while carving hard woods like lignum vitae. I don't use these things as often as I should, but I strongly recommend that you do.

EXPENDABLES

Sandpaper: Here is a product that has outgrown its name. Once it was quite literally a piece of paper with sand glued on it. Today it consists of many abrasives, such as aluminum oxide or carborundum, applied electrostatically to various backings in such a manner that the sharp points point upward. The change took place about twenty years ago and yet many people still do not realize it.

Backing material has changed also. Paper backing, still available and inexpensive, is fine for large flat areas, but it cracks and wears out quickly when folded or bent. Cloth backing is best for working in tight or curved places. I recommend wet-or-dry paper, which means it can be used with or without moisteners. It costs a little more but it is much better.

The numbering scheme for this product has also been changed. What once was known as 4/0 and 6/0 is now graded 150A and 220A, respectively. Grades range from 100 through 400. A beginner should have a selection of 100, which is coarse, 180, 220 and 280. This will be adequate. 320 and 400 are used on very hard woods and have more of a polishing effect.

Never buy cheap sandpaper. Never buy it in the dimestore. First, that is the most expensive way to buy it. Second, it is an inferior product. Third, they do not stock the finer grades. Even hardware stores rarely have an adequate selection. Many housewives who like to finish furniture read in the instructions that they should finish with fine sandpaper. They think 150A is it. It isn't. Many stores will look her right in the eye and say there is no such thing as 280, because they don't sell it. Go to a good abrasive supplier. You will find one in the phone book of any large town.

Although the name is a misnomer, I will use the term "sandpaper" in this book because the connotation is clear.

Steel Wool: This product retains the old numbering scheme of 3, 2, 1, 0 (pronounced "ought"), 2/0, 3/0 and 4/0. Buy 2/0 and 3/0 to start with. These are fine sizes and may be hard to find in the average hardware store, but a heavier grade will mar your work. Steel wool is better on hard woods than sandpaper and leaves less residue in the material. It leaves a grimy discoloration on soft woods, however, by depositing steel grit in the pores of the wood. A lot of amateur furniture finishers suffer with dull finishes because they leave this residue on the wood which eventually corrodes and spoils the finish.

Steel wool is reusable, but always keep it tightly closed in glass or metal containers. When it is dirty it is highly susceptible to spontaneous combustion.

SUMMARY

You don't need to buy a lot of tools, but what you buy should be of the finest quality. Take care of them and they will take care of you.

If you are following our suggested reading plan, skip ahead now to the second part of the next chapter, the section called "More on Wood."

TWO

MATERIAL

WHY WOOD?

THE only material worked in this book is wood. Why wood, when the popular media today are plastics or fabricated metals? That is a valid question.

The quickest answer is that there are several different art media and you should try them all, particularly when you are young. This book explains how to use wood. Other books help with other materials. Study them, too, but take one thing at a time and learn it well.

Art in wood has been around for a long time, dating back to an Egyptian boat decorated about 4000 B.C. It has been in and out of fashion ever since. I personally think that it is coming back into favor again, but like all old men I tend to think that the things I like are coming back.

I would never try to convince anybody that one medium is better than another. That is not true. One medium is probably more appealing to you, the artist, and to you, the observer. This is natural.

One real advantage of working in wood is that you do it all. You're not involved with dealing with a metal caster or a welder or a finisher. The last chapter showed that your tools can be relatively inexpensive and easily bought. You don't need an elaborate work area either.

The most obvious difference between wood and other media is its natural character, its color, grain and feel. Nature creates fantastic designs in wood. We will talk more about that later on.

Fig. 8. Mother and Child, Cherry, 12". Cherry is gorgeous wood. The color is rich, the grain flowing and the workability just right for a beginner.

WHAT TO BUY

Getting wood is hard for a beginner. He doesn't even know what kind to get. A beginner should use native wood. He should get a fairly hard wood. Soft wood requires exceedingly sharp tools to yield sharp lines. Unfortunately, most beginners go out and get a piece of white pine, which is very available, very soft and almost impossible to work with because it won't cut properly. Extremely hard wood is also difficult to manipulate at first.

The best bet is walnut, cherry or mahogany. You won't need a large piece; four inches thick by a foot square is fine. You can saw that in half and have two workable blocks.

Learn this fact: wood is where you find it. As you progress in your

Fig. 9. Saint Joan (After G. B. Shaw), Walnut, 18″. The beauty of American Walnut is obvious. Contrast the stoic feel of this piece with Fig. 10.

craft many varied sources of supply will suggest themselves to you to be ferreted out. At present, however, just look around. I started in lumber yards and woodlots. Fireplace wood is logical because the wood has been cut to a workable size and has already been somewhat seasoned.

If you go to a lumberyard look at the four-inch boards. Expect to pay about $1.25 a board foot. You will discover soon enough that buying wood from commercial suppliers is expensive, so start small and cheaply. Use local wood from old barns and fences. Almost any wood is amenable to sculpturing with few exceptions. Mesquite dulls tools, for example, and redwood splinters. Use any local hard wood that is easy to find and of a suitable size.

You know enough now to get through a piece or two, so I suggest that you skip the rest of this chapter and begin Chapter Three which will help you through your first piece. Good luck.

MORE ON WOOD

The first part of this chapter told you how to get a decent chunk or two of wood. If you continue in this craft you will eventually tire of going to the same fireplace wood dealer and hunting through his stacks for the same kind of log that you worked on the last time and the time before that. You will want diversity. That is the joy of working in this medium. It has diversity. If I stayed with one species I would probably dry up, but each piece brings a new look and a new challenge with it. This is the true reward for working in wood: the infinite variety of the material.

FLAWS

This infinite variety also implies a lack of a standard, an absence of perfection. This is true. With variety come flaws, and you will need to learn to recognize them and cope with them.

When a tree is alive and standing it is full of water. The amount of moisture that a full-grown tree pumps through its body is staggering. When this tree is felled it begins to lose its moisture. If the wood dries unevenly, as it almost always does, the entrapped water will cause stresses and strains on the fiber structure, ultimately creating cracks. Cracking is always a potential threat.

It can be controlled by allowing the moisture to leave the wood

Fig. 10. John Brown, Walnut, 26″. Saint Joan (Fig. 9) and old John Brown have markedly different moods, yet they are both embodied in all-purpose walnut, a wood faithful to almost any design.

evenly and at a moderate rate. Residual water will always reside in wood no matter how slowly it is dried, seldom going under 8 per cent by volume, so the danger is always present. Unequal drying is the villain. Wood dries faster on the outside, for example, and it dries faster on the cut ends. Contact with a table or floor will suck out moisture unequally. Breezes and radiation act in the same way. A larger piece is more subject to cracking because of the greater disparity between the inner and the outer forces. As a consequence the powerful force of nature rips apart the wood to release its water.

A question of every sculptor or patron is, "How do you repair cracks?" Well, you don't. The crack comes from the moisture on the inside trying to get out. Fill the outer crack and the water is still inside trying to get out. The wood constantly expands and contracts and the filler merely aggravates the flaw. All but imperceptible cracks are irreparable.

I work on the principle that I want my wood well settled. I season my wood supply the way the Steinway Company seasons its soundboards, the heart of their pianos. They subject them to the worst possible conditions, leaving them in the back lot through ice and snow and rain. After a suitable time they are cut and patched and ready to use. Whatever was going to happen to them has happened. I do the same. I lose wood, but when I am ready to use what is left I know that it is good.

Rapid change is the enemy of well-seasoned wood. Changing the storage environment from an icy back lot to the inside of a highly heated low-humidity workshop is bad. Cutting too drastically into a large piece of wood is bad. That converts the middle to the outside. The pressures of the locked-in moisture change dramatically, setting up new stress lines. Give the wood a little time to adjust in both cases.

Hard wood cracks more easily than soft wood because of the rigid cellular walls. All ebony over three inches in diameter will have cracks. If the wood is expensive and is prone to cracking, the ends can be sealed with unthinned shellac temporarily to restrain sudden change. I do this with about 15 to 20 per cent of my supply.

I recently disregarded my own precepts with a large piece of monkeypod. It was from a well-seasoned tree, but it had been residing in a tropical climate. It was shipped abruptly to my workshop. If it had been left alone for a while it would have adjusted. I wanted to use it right away, alas, and I tried to fix it so it wouldn't crack. That was my first mistake. My second was to turn the furnace on in the fall. Air blew

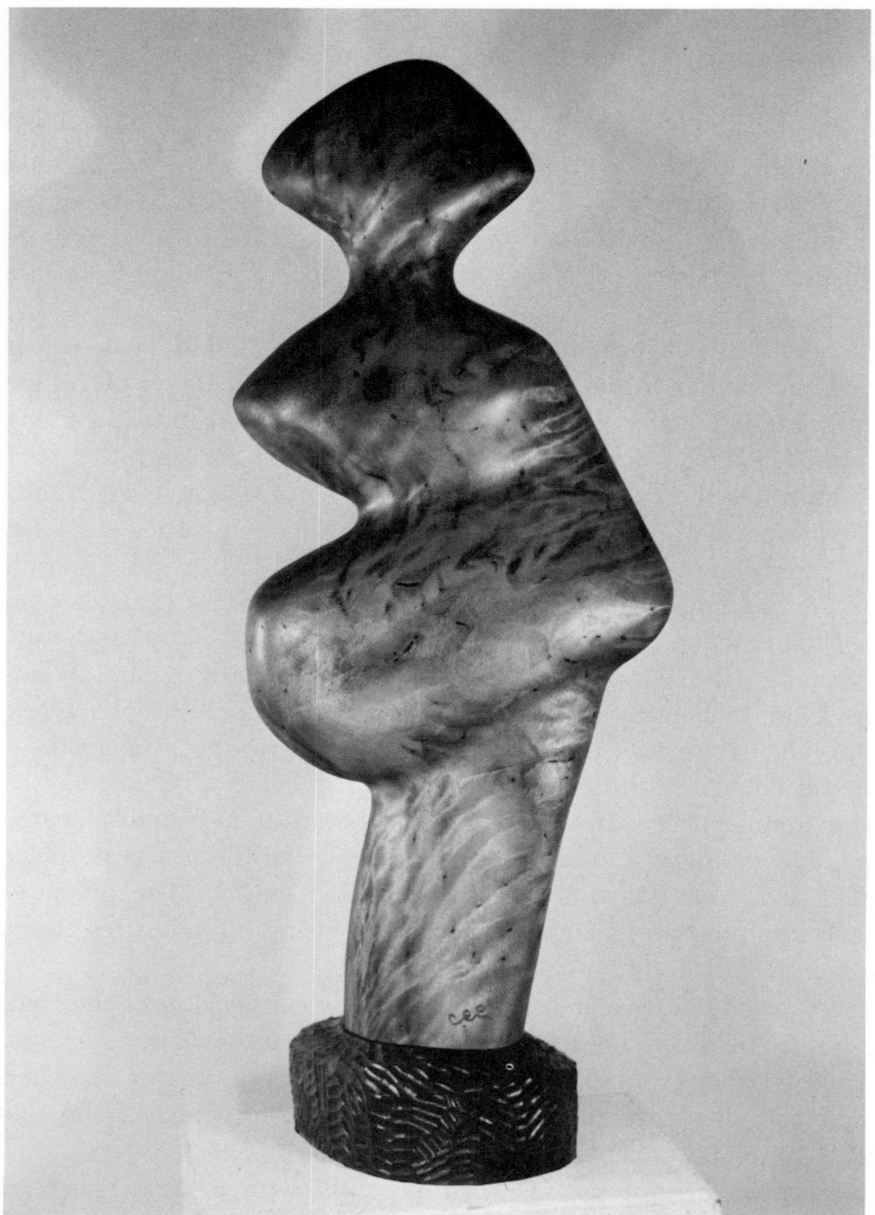

Fig. 11. Earth Mother, Curly Robusta, 40″. The translucent surface quality of this golden red exotic is unreal. A thousand lights seem to gleam from it as you pass by.

across one corner of the piece from the hot air duct and made a tiny crack worse. All I can do now is put a little oil on the crack and slow it down. It is there because I thought I could outwit the natural way of nature. I always lose this contest, and so will you.

DRYING

You have heard of kiln-dried wood. This is a controlled method of speeding up nature's process. Four-inch thicknesses are the normal maximum for kiln drying, taking about three months. We have tried drying five-inch pieces of walnut over a six-month period but they were full of flaws. You usually have to buy pre-dried wood as the kiln service is not easy to find.

A rule of thumb for natural drying is one year per inch radius. This holds true up to four inches of radius, after which the time scale lengthens. This is only a guideline. Linden, for example, can be used immediately due to the inherent structure of the wood. Mahogany dries faster than walnut as the interleaving grain decreases cracking. If you want to dry your own wood just rack it up in the garage so the air can get to it and don't worry about the heat.

OTHER FLAWS

Collapse: One flaw difficult to find is called a collapse. This is often caused by too-rapid kiln drying that does not allow the heat to penetrate into the wood, although it happens naturally, also. The wood pulls away from itself leaving a hollow spot inside the log that does not show on the surface. Experience will teach you to locate collapses by tapping the wood. Collapsed areas have a different hollow sound. As you are working, continually tap to learn to recognize this sound. Tapping can only be learned through experience. It comes gradually, but it will save you hours of agony. After ten or twelve years you will be good at it. Within a month or so after you begin you will detect three-fourths of the flaws, but you won't be able to find the dangerous ones. That takes time.

Holes: Rocks buried in wood are always hard to find. They have a different sound, however, so if you hear something strange go on into the wood and get it out. It leaves a little hollow between it and the wood, along with a dirty discoloration.

Lead bullets are apparently antiseptic as they leave no hollow spot. It is amazing how many bullets you will find. I find about one a month. It may have been shot fifty years ago and the wood grown completely around it. Lead is bad enough, but you will really get mad when you discover a steel-jacketed bullet with your best chisel. It invariably costs you a chipped chisel.

Holes caused by budding rootforms or insects are a problem, too. Occasionally you will find a live bug in the piece you are working on. If you do, put some carbon tetrachloride in a little oil squirt can and squirt it into the hole. Adjust the wood so that gravity will carry the fumes downward. It always works. Museums use this technique for antique furniture. Please be careful, though, as carbon tetrachloride is dangerous for humans to breathe as well as for insects.

It is best not to try and plug holes. If a knot should fall out or if the spot isn't prominently a part of your design you might get away with repairing it. You do this by drilling a round hole. Take a piece of the same wood and round it with a slight taper. Apply Elmer's Glue. Drive it in and cut it off. It will look like a knot because the end grain will show, but it will detract no more than a knot would.

Learn as much as you can about these flaws. The average beginner takes a piece of wood and the first thing he does is put a design in it. After he starts sculpturing he finds a flaw. His prearranged design is dead. He must learn to clean up the wood first before he designs in it. In a real sense sculpturing is a two-step operation. First, clean up the wood, keeping designs from your mind so you won't prejudicially ignore a flaw that will hurt you later on. Only when the wood is clean can you design the piece. The beginner is going to ignore this, and he is going to waste time. As most wood is flawed, you must calculate which flaws you can live with. Cleaning the wood takes about 20 per cent of your time when you are good. The beginner won't take that long because he won't be trying to figure out how to best remove the flaw. He'll just chop it out and waste some wood. He'll finish quickly, but he won't know what he is doing. I think you will agree that until you know what you are doing you are not good.

ACQUISITION

Obtaining wood is exhilarating and depressing by turns, but it is

Fig. 12. Lonely Crowd, Ebony and Avodire, 17″. The color contrast of these two exotics helps enforce the theme of separation in this piece. The apparent absence of grain in the ebony figures also aided the sense of anonymity. This piece done in cherry or walnut would not be the same at all.

always expensive. There are just so many old barns to be torn down that are made of just the kind of wood you need. Eventually you will want to turn to a commercial source. A few of these are listed in the Appendix. Don't hesitate to use them. Finding and keeping track of suppliers is not easy, by the way, so the Appendix should be helpful to you. As you get into the business more and more, the tracking down of new sources and suppliers becomes a hobby in itself.

There are three geographical categories of wood for mainland Americans: (1) domestic wood; (2) foreign wood; (3) Hawaiian wood. I strongly advise that you begin with domestic wood, assuming you live in the continental United States. There are a number of reasons for this, the prime one being: wood is where you find it. It is relatively cheap and readily available. One needn't wait months for a shipment only to receive the wrong wood. You know exactly what it is when you trip over it.

Domestically, cherry and walnut are generally available and are both outstanding woods. They don't have the advantage of being exotic, which sends quivers up and down your customer's spine, but they are perfectly beautiful woods in appearance and workability. They are similar to one another, with cherry being a little harder and a little more closely grained. One disadvantage of walnut is its typically large size. Walnut trees are big and usually require a lot of sectioning to get pieces of workable size. Mahogany is another good wood for beginners. Its interlapping grain is interesting and a useful lesson in chisel handling.

Exotic woods are expensive and difficult to acquire. Why bother with them? Unfortunately, our country's supply of wood suitable for sculpture is fast diminishing. Even walnut is becoming scarce. Also, exotic wood

Fig. 13. New Mexico Landscape, Myrtlewood Burl, 19". The violent grain structure of the burl accentuates the ruggedness of the design.

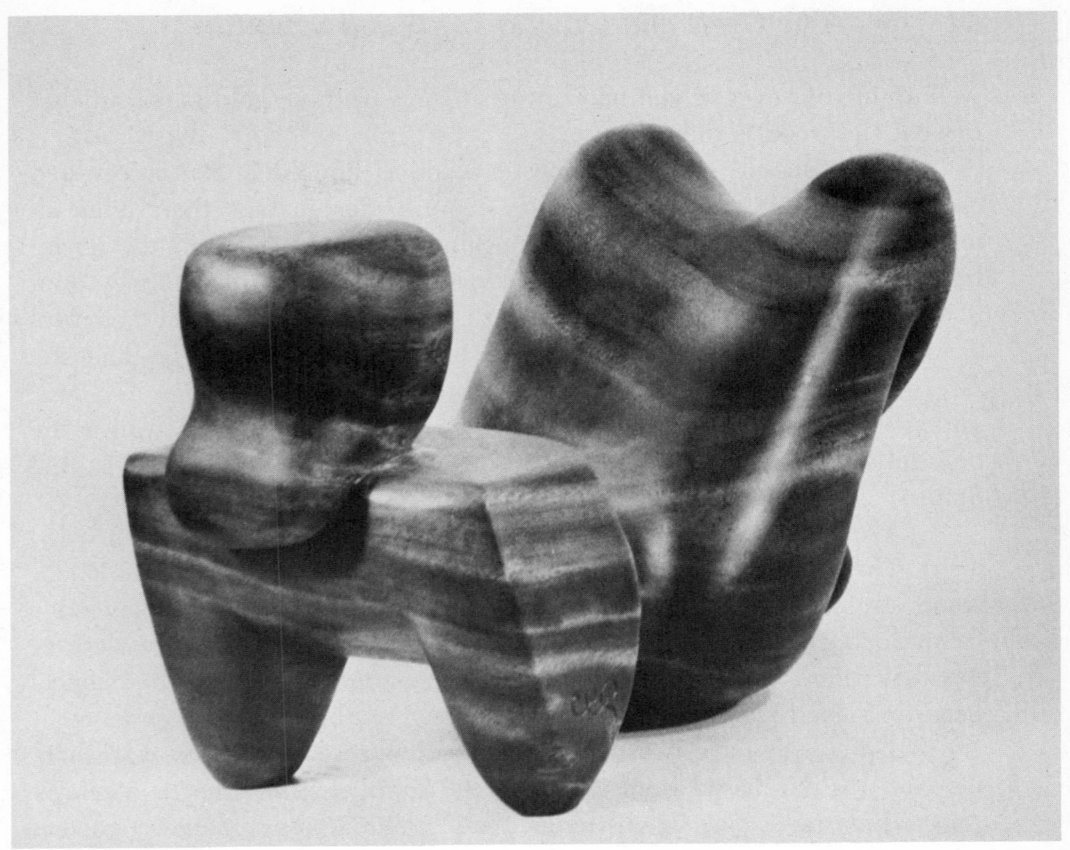

Fig. 14. Reclining Woman, Monkey Pod, 8″. This is a good example of the vibrant quality of a very interesting Hawaiian wood.

is different—completely different. Each kind must be studied for its particular assets and disadvantages. As you develop you will feel the need and desire to expand, to learn and to experiment with new ideas in new media. Working in ebony is as different from working in teak as pastels differ from oil. It adds to your vocabulary as an artist. You will discover for yourself that rosewood resists lateral movement, for example, or that teak is brittle and will split, that zebrawood's interweaving grain won't allow it to split, yet it can be both delicate and tough. This sort of knowledge enables you to become a better sculptor.

When you do use exotics you must force yourself to select that type of wood which is best for your idea, not that which is cheapest. If you are going to buy it you may as well use it to its best advantage. Sure, the tears well up in your eyes as you hack away at some of these gold bars, but that is what the wood is there for.

What should we do? Domestic wood is limited in its variety and exotic wood is expensive and hard to acquire. Fortunately, there is an alternative. I am not in the wood-selling business. I have absolutely no interest, financial or personal, in the Hawaiian wood industry, but they offer a happy solution to our problem in the form of a half-dozen beautiful carving woods. There is no duty to pay. Instead of $5 stamps, the domestic rate will fly a letter there in no time. The language is the same as yours, and so is the money. As long as the world remains unsettled Hawaii is the only satisfactory source of unusual woods for us in the continental United States.

Wood Chart: Every book on wood or wood sculpture boasts a wood chart. There has to be a wood chart or it wouldn't be a proper book about wood. Unfortunately I have never garnered any appreciable knowledge from wood charts. The main reason, I believe, is the amazing variety of wood, within one species, one location, or even one log. This is the magical beauty of wood as a medium. Each new piece is a brand new experience.

I presently have two batches of Brazilian rosewood in my workshop. One lot was purchased from a commercial supplier. The other is a pile of rejected marimba bars, of all things, that I came across somehow (wood is where you find it). The neophyte would never think them to be of the same species. One is very dark, the other is light. I imagine the light wood grew at high altitudes with low precipitation and in soil rich in minerals.

There are over forty different species of walnut in the United States alone. It grows in highlands and lowlands. Even on the same tree one limb might be one color, the trunk another, and the burl—if any—another. The variations are endless.

Ebony in Mexico is light brown, for example, and is darker brown in the Congo. The deep black ebony with which you are probably familiar is from the Guinea Coast of Africa. It is all ebony, but it is all different. The same point can be made about grain, or strength, or workability, ad infinitum. Commercial concerns, such as lumber dealers, can use charts because they order so many million board feet at a time. The averages will apply. The individual sculptor who just orders one or two little chunks of a particular wood cannot depend upon the averages. He can't set his power saws to accept the mean or prepare his milling machines for nominal strength. Instead he finds himself staring at one very individual piece of wood which may or may not (the laws of probability saying not) be an average piece of walnut, or ebony, or whatever. Don't be misled by charts, including ours.

Why have a chart if they are worthless? Aside from "being necessary in a book about wood," it will give you a *general* idea of what to look for in different species. Our chart, found in the Appendix, is in three sections: the domestic and exotic sections are not elaborate, but since Hawaiian woods are a bargain with which you are probably unfamiliar, more detail is found in that section, thanks to my friend, Mr. Myron Wold. The only way that you are really going to get to know these woods is to work them and work them over again.

Felt: The little piece of felt on the bottom of a finished work is often unnoticed. If so, it has been applied properly. Its color should blend the piece with its supporting surface. Buy various rolls of felt and apply the right color for the right situation with glue. The felt, aside from acting as a transition point, prevents scratching.

Proceed now to Chapter Four if you are following our suggested reading plan, as you have already made the mask in Chapter Three. Now you are ready to learn what sort of design you should make with your newly acquired skill at sculpturing in wood.

THREE

THE MASK

CRAFTSMANSHIP

The first section of this book is about "craftsmanship." What is a craftsman? A standard dictionary definition reads:

> "A person, as a writer or artist, skilled in the mechanics of his craft."

That is not very exciting, is it? But it says it all. "Skilled," "mechanics," "craft"; these are three key words. We all think we know what "skilled" means, and we probably do. "Mechanics" will throw the dilettantes among us a little off stride. Mechanics sounds like work. It doesn't sound like creating, or beauty, or Art at all. The same applies to "craft." Craft is beadwork, or hemstitching. What happened to Art? We want to express our Great Thought in the Realm of Art. Don't burden us with this mucky business about mechanics and craft.

The painful truth, however, is that if you want your great idea to be expressed it must be through the mechanical skill of your craft. You will simply have to learn how to manipulate the wood before you can expect the wood to manipulate your idea into art. An artist friend of mine has a succinct definition of craftsmanship: "It means I can put the paint where I want it." That little statement is colloquial, but there is a lot of meaning hiding in it.

Some fools worship skill at the expense of its partner, creativity. Others make the opposite mistake. They are both wrong. Your skill should let your idea come out. Skill without creativity is nothing. It is polished and dull. On the other hand, good ideas poorly executed are a crime against nature. You owe it to yourself and to your viewers to develop the ability to be able to do exactly what you have in mind. If not, you have to stand around and tell everyone how good it would have been if you could just have captured the image of your mind on the wood. I personally believe in craftsmanship. If the piece is not well done it is marred. I've judged a lot of shows and I've seen few good pieces that weren't skillfully done. That is why we are learning how to handle the tools before we get into the masterpiece business.

Sculpturing, after all, is hard work. There is no sense in going into it or continuing with it unless you really want to do it. To do so would be drudgery. Probe your sensibilities during your first few pieces and ask yourself how you really feel about the task. Either you will want to continue or you won't. In the latter case please stop and save yourself some trouble.

Also, don't expect to make steady progress. As in most learning situations, you will spurt up, plateau, sink, and then spurt up again. The neophyte who thinks otherwise is in for a headache about his fifth piece. By then he will be applying all his newly won knowledge at once, bobble, and probably create his worst piece. Learning is just like inspiration, with which I personally have had dismal luck; it doesn't come all at once in a blinding flash and it doesn't come easily. Plan to work at least one hour each night. After you become more accomplished you can work for two minutes and get two minutes work done, but particularly at first you should spend a decent chunk of time at this new thing. The artistic muscle needs regular exercise, too.

WHY A MASK?

There are good reasons for making a mask your first piece. It is well to start with a relatively shallow surface, allowing the concept of the third dimension to slowly emerge. Mass is a crucial need of sculpture, as we shall elaborate upon later, but you are not adjusted to thinking in the round yet. A mask is basically two-dimensional, with its flat back hanging against a wall, and that is why it is a good place to start. I am talking about the African or Indian masks that you have seen in pictures or at the museum. They allow the third dimension to insinuate itself enough to nudge your mind to think about it.

The ordinary beginner gets hopelessly bogged down in rules of anatomy and other technicalities, both real and imagined. With a mask he can ignore these problems and concentrate on learning tool control. Even better, he can use his imagination. If he knows nothing about masks, or is afraid to use his creativity, he can get some books from the library for a guide. He can make a mask any shape he wants. He won't get tangled up with reality, he will begin thinking in the round without becoming immersed in it, and he will be creating instead of copying. That is a pretty good bargain for a first piece.

SELECTING THE WOOD

The French recipe for roast rabbit begins, "First you catch a rabbit." The same theory applies here; first you get the wood. Get a piece as seasoned, meaning dry, as possible. Try to get a piece of walnut, or cherry, or mahogany, or any similar wood of fairly hard and interesting grain. We want a piece roughly two or three inches thick by a foot by a half-foot. The measurements certainly don't have to be exact. I do suggest that they should be rectangular for your first mask so that you don't get completely lost.

Check the wood for flaws. Make it as free from flaws as possible (Fig. 15). Your chances of doing well the first time are poor. If you start with a flawed piece your chances are even worse.

If it has a knot in an important area, decide whether you can incorporate it into your design or whether you should take it out. If you must take it out, do so thoroughly and cautiously so that there is no trace of the flaw to hamper your already revised design. A flaw is going to detract from your design whether you like it or not. If there is a bad crack on the surface you had better chip away at either side of it until you are at its base. Only then will you know exactly how much wood you will have left for your design. Don't forget the sides and bottom of your block either. Even the back, which will lie unseen against the wall, should be examined for any deep flaws that may go almost all the way through the wood without surfacing on the other side. One blow with the chisel and the crack might surface on the front of your once beautiful design. If in doubt, cut it out. If the surface is exceedingly rough or barked, you might want to do some preliminary smoothing passes across it. This is covered in more detail later on.

After the wood is clean and the damaging flaws are apparently gone, you are ready to put in the design.

Fig. 15. The raw material for the mask is Koa from Hawaii. Mine will be a little more adventuresome than yours, but I am attempting to evade the imitation of primitive sculpture so commonly found in mask design. The heavy scar on the side will have to be removed before I even consider my design.

DESIGN

To reiterate, if this is your first effort you are going to want to make a masterpiece. It is only human, but forget it. You don't know how and you are going to get yourself all bogged down in details. You will learn much more if you will concentrate on making a simple statement. Keep it simple and eliminate details.

Take a piece of paper the size of your material, or mark off a rectangle on your workbench with chalk. Remember, this is a mask, unfettered by anatomical restrictions or almost any other rules of reality.

Chalk in the basic shapes and locations of the nose, eyes and mouth, if you have chosen to portray them. You can make your man noseless if you wish, or make him all nose. I do suggest that you keep the left and right sides of the mask symmetrical. This guards against the famous "asymmetric cop-out" in case the piece doesn't work out the way you had hoped. You will shortly learn that the exact control of your tools is not easy. Making a regular design will arbitrarily force you to put certain lines in certain places, even if it happens to be a difficult place. Better that you learn this knack now rather than shifting your designs around and hoping to be known as an asymmetric artist.

My mask is not going to be similar on either side, but trust me in this. I have made my share of masks, and there is nothing wrong with putting a nose off-center if you really want it off-center. The question is, did you really want it off-center. Picasso, I am convinced, knows to a fraction just how far from reality his distortions roam. The beginner doesn't—yet.

Run your design right to the edge. You paid for the wood and you should use it. This is particularly important later on when you will be using costly material. Most new people are used to seeing borders, even around sketches, so they leave a little room at the edge. Don't. You will mutter more than once that there just isn't enough wood for your idea. This is not true, of course. If the graphic artist can work with a limited two-dimensional piece of paper or canvas, we can manage with a thick piece of wood.

It is not necessary to spend a great deal of time on these preliminary drawings. There should be no clamor from the neighbors to tear the bench top off and send it to the Guggenheim. Drawing, per se, is not particularly important at this stage, especially if you have a good mind's eye that can retain your idea in your head. When I began I did quite meticulous drawings, but now I usually dash off a few guidelines right on the wood. There are three reasons for this. First, your drawing is flat. As you proceed you begin to see in the round. The drawing, by definition, will lose its validity. Second, if you tie yourself to a specific plan you will have lost all ability to change in case of an unexpected flaw or a tragic slip of the chisel at a crucial spot. Third, if you copy a drawing into a piece of wood you might as well copy a Picasso as yours and do a better bad piece. You halt all creative thought when you copy. Although we are talking skills here, it is imperative that you never get in the way of your creative juices. Keep the drawing general.

Now transfer the outline and general placement of the major features onto the wood. Pencil or ball-point pen are fine for making detailed lines, but you are making general lines. Keep it loose. Don't bother to define the structure of the eye, for example, any more than to decide whether it will be a hole or a hump.

CHISEL AND GOUGE

Before shaping your design, you must have a solid way to hold the wood. Either the bench vise or two-by-four arrangement mentioned in Chapter One will do. One warning: the quickest way to take the life out of your tempered steel chisels and gouges is to bang them against the steel jaws of a vise. Pad several thicknesses of wood and paperboard between the material and the holder (Fig. 2, Item X). Then if you slip only your pride is damaged, and it comes cheaper than tools.

At last you can begin. Start with a one-inch #5 gouge, the big one with the slight bow in the blade. Hold it in your weak hand. Hold the mallet in your strong hand.* Your mask will probably, but not necessarily, have rounded edges to make use of the third dimension, so start by removing some wood around the upper edge just to get the feel of the tool in your hand. Concentrate on two things: the grain of the wood and the cutting edge of the tool. Often you can't, but always try to cut with the grain. If you don't you will tear into the wood, leaving gashes and flaws that are dangerous and hard to repair. The more you work, the more aware you become of the grain and its vagaries. Some woods have relatively straight grain, some have cockeyed but parallel grain. Mahogany has a wavy interlapping grain that folds over upon itself. Always watch the

*I am right-handed, but in deference to you left-handers I will use this weak/strong distinction throughout the text:

right-handers—right hand is strong, left hand is weak.
left-handers—left hand is strong, right hand is weak.

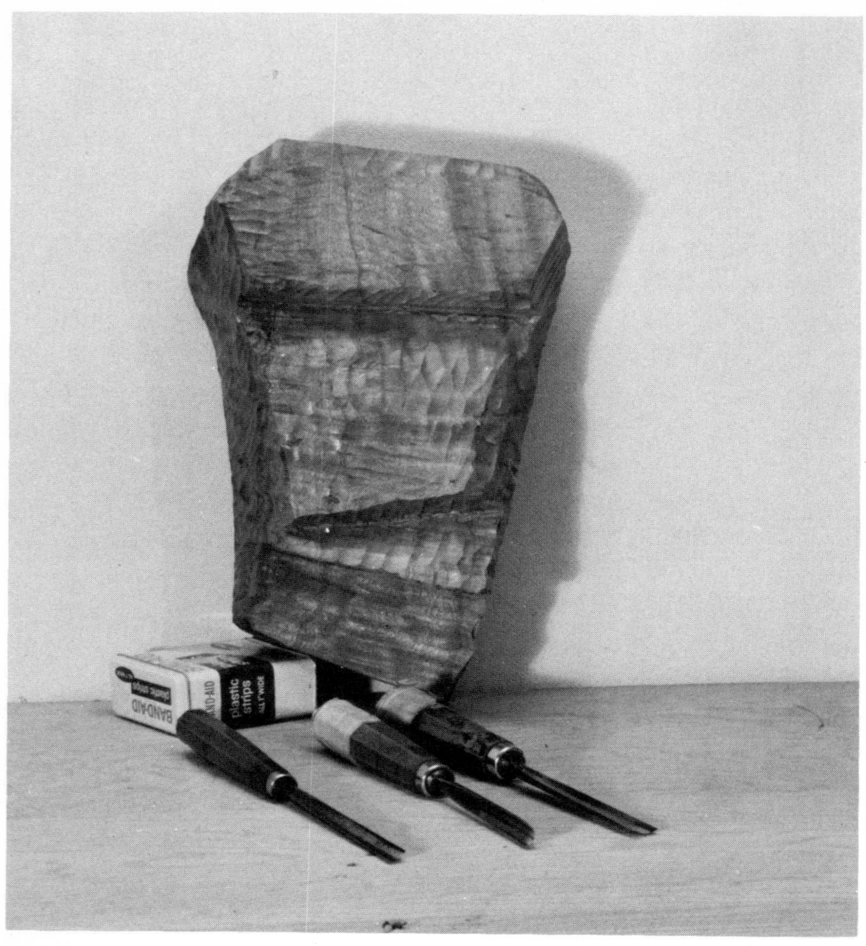

Fig. 16. My mask after laying out the major forms. So far I have used only the deep gouge and two medium gouges. The Band-Aid box is always being put to good use.

grain and cut in the direction of the emerging grain as it surfaces. If you must you can cut cross-grain at a 90-degree angle. When you do this you must be more careful. When you really become adept you may cut against the grain occasionally. Please don't contemplate that trick yet. As you progress you will know when the chisel is riding the grain just right, and a lot of your success will be due to this simple knack.

There is no "perfect" angle at which to hold the gouge against the wood. You can turn the gouge over and use it upside down if you are careful. Anything is legal that works. Use what feels the best and cuts the wood in the manner that you want it cut.

One practice should be discouraged. Do not hold the blade at such an angle or hit the handle so hard that the points of the gouge are buried in the wood. You can damage both blade and wood by going in too deeply.

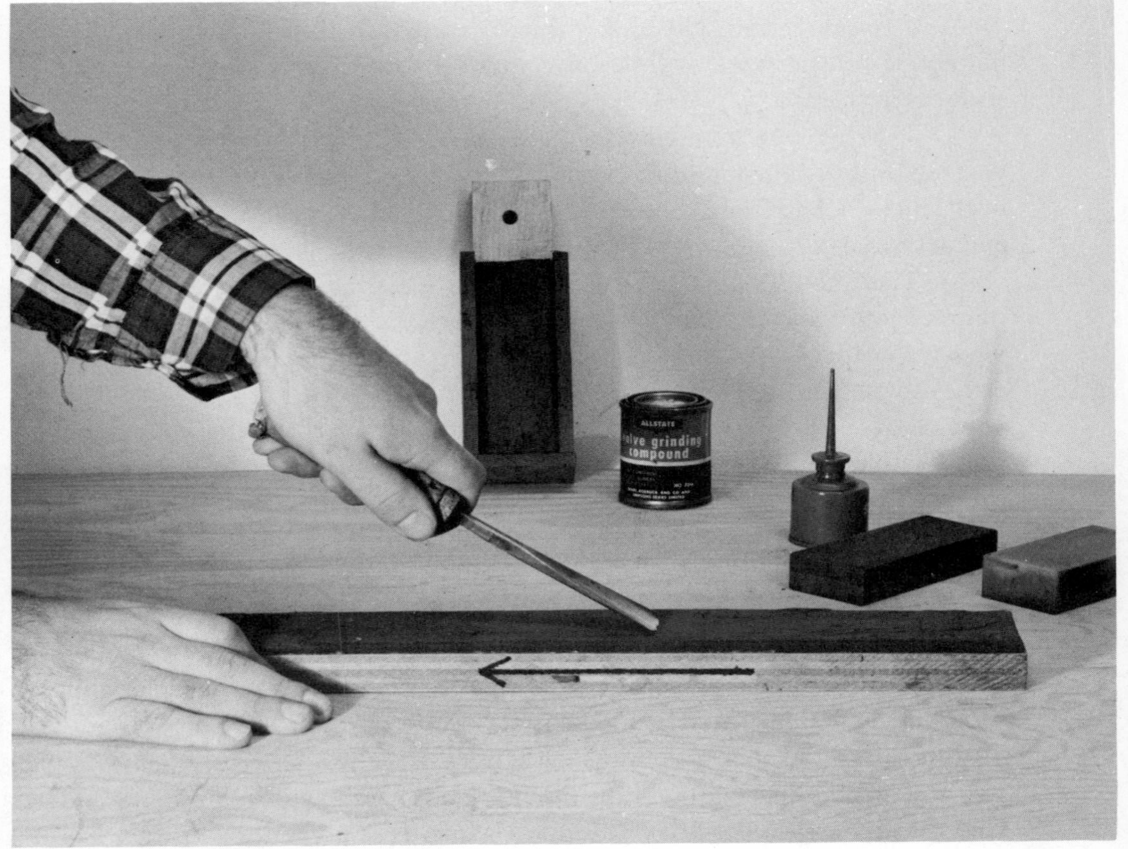

Fig. 17. I first ran across this honing idea in Mexico years ago. I tried to find out what the elements of the little board leaning in the background were. The best we could decipher was a leather strap covered with a mixture of soap and graphite. In desperation the craftsman gave it to me. I successfully used it and the larger one for years before graduating to a grindstone (covered in last part of Chapter One). I found that adding plenty of valve-grinding compound helps. Pull the tool firmly in the direction of the arrow, rotating the gouge blade for evenness. Whetstones are also fine for honing, but the Arkansas stone on the right cost $25. The carborundum stone is less. Be sure to apply oil to the stones to wash away the chips.

Occasionally you will have to do this, but when you do, be aware that you have been warned.

Don't hit too hard. If you insist on hitting too hard you will cause yourself many hardships. Some of them:

1. The tool edge won't hold up under the constant barrage. You will be sharpening tools more often than you are hitting them.

2. Your mallet arm will be lifting and dropping a hundred thousand times. If you do it naturally and without stress you will be able to last indefinitely. If you push you will become physically tired, no matter how young and strong you are.

3. When you hit a chisel it must be under control to assure safety to yourself and to your intended design. A misguided gentle tap isn't going to hurt much. A bad bang, however, could cause much pain, both physically and aesthetically.

There is a "right way" to swing the mallet. Even a gentle tap requires energy and you will want to conserve energy. The worst way, obviously, would be to pound into the ceiling directly overhead with your arm fully extended. The answer is to let the mallet fall with gravity. Hold your elbow next to your body and use it as a fulcrum, keeping your upper arm relatively still. While the size of the chip is not important at the start, the pace is. Develop a nice steady rhythm. Change it periodically to keep loose, but a steady tap-tapping is the secret to progress.

The beginner invariably has trouble with chisel control. Expect this and don't feel too bad. Just take your time and pay attention to what you are doing and use little rabbit punches with the mallet. If you think you aren't getting anywhere, check with a friend who is also learning sculpture and thinks that banging is the only way. Measure his progress against yours and then you will feel better.

Turn the piece around in the vise when you need to. Stop and analyze it and work on the other side for a while. It is a good idea to work all around the piece anyway, as we will discuss in a later chapter. When you think you have rounded the edge smooth, stand back and take a look.

I'll bet you have rounded the edge all right, but you have left at least half the back thickness and most of the front untouched. Welcome to the third dimension. The face should start rounding toward the middle from the very back. If you are only going to use one inch of thickness on your two-inch-thick board, you have selected the wrong board. Go around again and really bring those edges down. Your mask is not conforming to anatomy, but probably will have a forehead that recedes, a chin and neck that slope down, and cheeks that slope in from the ears. If so, you can cut these areas away, leaving untouched places in the middle for the protruding features. Remember to leave the back flat so that it will lie flat against the wall. Now see how much more wood you can take off.

If you find a place that is fairly flat and broad you may want to use the one-inch flat chisel. Its flat surface is smoother than the gouge and will help you smooth the area more quickly. Generally, you can cut deeper and faster with a gouge and smoother with a chisel. The blade width is dictated by the surface. The bigger the area and the less important the margin of safety each imply using a bigger tool. Why? Because it is faster. It is as simple as that. No matter how big the gouge, however, remember not to bury the points.

It is time for a few reminders. First, don't hit that chisel handle too hard. You have plenty of time if each blow is under control, but you will never have time to correct the results of one blow out of control.

Second, are your tools still sharp? If you find them dragging or tending to tear or splinter the wood, then it is time to resharpen them. You will resharpen a lot, so you may as well learn to do it properly from the start.

Is your working surface rough? That means you are cutting against the grain. This is always dangerous. Watch the grain and keep your surface smooth. You might want to switch to a smaller-width tool to take off smaller bites.

Be sure and try to keep your work symmetrical. Work on one side a bit and then bring the other side down to the same plane. If the chisel keeps digging in, use the gouge. The little curve in the gouge allows it to gloss over the rough spots. Try to avoid any deep gashes that may fracture the wood. Always strive for a smooth surface so that you can tell just where you are.

HOLDING BLOCK

Your piece should be fairly rounded now and the major masses formed. You have probably noticed how difficult it is to work around the areas close to the jaws of the vise. It is imperative that the chisel blade not

Fig. 18. Attaching the holding block. Notice I have carefully marked on the mask the depth of the screws. The necessary drills and screws are pictured. Notice the tape to limit the depth of the smallest drill.

be smashed into the jaws, yet it is sometimes impossible to keep a good purchase on the material and carve effectively at the same time. The remedy is a holding block. We will attach a block on the back of the mask to hold it in the vise without damage.

Cut out a piece of wood a few inches thick and somewhat smaller than your mask. You will be fastening it to the mask in several places. Make sure the screws don't go through the mask. If in doubt, use several shorter screws for solidity. Aim for the thickest masses, such as the nose area. Drill several holes through the holding block at these support points. Select a drill size a bit larger than the diameter of the screw. Then drill down about an inch into these holes with a drill larger than the head of the screw. Drop the screws in place and tap them to mark the back of the mask. Then drill carefully the marked holes using a drill the size of the shank of the screw, so that only the threads will cut into the wood. Measure the screws carefully and put masking tape on the drill at exactly the length of penetration desired. Drill the holes just this far. Don't go in too fast or you will push the tape back and lose the proper length.

If the wood is extremely hard use a drill a bit larger in diameter or the wood will fracture when you screw down the block. Also, run the hole a little deeper than the screw length so the excess chips will have a place to go. It would also be a good idea to run a slightly larger drill down about halfway to allow for the taper of the screwshank.

Turn down all the screws and boldly mark the block and the mask where the screws are to avert tragedy. Now you have a good solid holder that will allow you to continue sculpturing without damage to the chisel or to the piece.

RASPING

Try to bring each stage of development along all at once all over the piece. Common sense tells you this, and we will discuss it in detail later on, but you are learning how to handle tools now and not design concepts. Be a little tender with the detail lines from now on. Chances are you are coming along and the shiny chip surfaces left by the gouge are confusing your vision a bit. You just can't see where you are. It is time for shellac and the rasp.

Buy a pint of white shellac and mix some of it with shellac thinner or alcohol at a ratio of about one part shellac to ten parts thinner. Brush this mixture generously over your work area. This colors the wood and lets you see where you are. Water would do just as well except for the problem of opening the grain again. Let it dry for about fifteen minutes. Now you can see the topography much more easily. Rub off the excess moisture with a rag. Shellac is not as inflammable as other resin products so you don't need to worry about spontaneous combustion from the shellac rags. You can leave the brush sitting in the thinned shellac jar as it is too thin to cause gumming problems.

When the surface dries rasp down the high spots. Hold the rasp at one end and push down with your other hand on the other end. As you work try to move the rasp around so you won't create an unwanted flat place.

Fig. 19. This stage was reached before picking up the rasp. The chalk marks are temporary guidelines that I am constantly sketching in the wood. This skewed design was chosen as a challenge. I strongly suggest that a beginner's mask should be symmetrical.

Work all around and in different directions if you can. Don't try to remove a lot of wood with a rasp, as it takes longer and is less efficient than the gouge. It is meant for smoothing and not for cutting.

It is hard to master the chisel, particularly in softer woods. The rasp is relatively easy. So guard against yourself because you might be tempted to use the rasp as a crutch. You pretend that you are doing just as well with the rasp, but you are cheating yourself twice: first, you will end up with a slick piece of wood, all smoothed and curved without character; second, you will never learn how to use the chisel, a necessity with harder woods.

After rasping the chisel marks smooth you will have a lot of sawdust and debris on the work surface. You won't be able to see again. Apply another dose of thin shellac and you can now see where the chisel should go. This is a continuous operation, chiseling, rasping and shellacking, over and over again.

If you have more than one rasp, use the larger in large areas, the smaller in small. This is simply because the bigger rasp is faster and more economical. You will be making enough swipes with a rasp and bangs with a chisel so that the idea of economy of motion will become more and more appealing to you. As with chisels, the best way to use a rasp is the slow, easy way. This gives the wood time to cut rather than tear. It gives your

Fig. 20. This is a beginner's first attempt at sculpturing. He deeply sympathizes with your problems at this point, just after the first rasping. It is obvious here that maintaining symmetry of the left and right sides is not only demanding but elusive.

muscles, and your brain, a chance to follow exactly what is going on. Take it easy and get more done.

Already you can see the advantage of having several tools. You can get by with the basics, but it takes longer. Just as the garage mechanic needs more tools than the shade-tree mechanic, the more involved you become in sculpture the more tools you will want and need to become at all efficient.

DETAIL

After several chisel-shellac-rasp cycles you should find yourself getting close to the cruciality of your piece, where one poorly hit chisel blade could create instant distaster. The basic tool skills remain unchanged, but their proper control becomes much more important.

Look at your piece as a design now. First check and make sure that you really have used those few inches of third dimension. Is it rounded enough, or should you get out the chisel and bring the edges down some more. I'll bet they could use it. Don't feel bad, as a flat surface is any beginner's problem. This is a good time to check the symmetry of your mask, also. Again, don't feel bad if you find that you will have to alter one side dramatically. If you don't do it now it simply won't be right and you won't have learned a thing unless you are the type that likes to cheat on yourself. Please don't make the opposite mistake of taking off one side to match the other, overshooting a bit and proceeding to do the same on the other side. Sometimes prudence is the better part of exactitude.

Flaws, always a problem, are even more so now. You must decide what flaws you can live with and what you can't. If you are going to leave a flaw or a knot in the piece you must incorporate it into your design, because it *is* in your design whether you admit it or not. It is going to be there working anyway, so you should try to make it work for you. An unwanted flaw is like a little black smudge on a clean piece of paper. Ask someone what he sees and he will say, "I see a little black smudge right there." The same applies to wood flaws. Always remove them when you first see them, or they will worsen.

Most people are in the process of making more flaws rather than repairing flaws as they approach completion of a piece. Often I put my mallet down and use both hands on the chisel, one pushing and one guiding. This adds control in the fine spots. You will invent several tricks for extra control as you progress, and this is the time to use them. It is most disappointing to work on a piece for three or four weeks only to destroy it at the end. When I get near the end of a piece I work at not making problems.

You may find yourself in a tight spot where you must cut against the grain. Go ahead, but go lightly. Your tools must be sharp and you must get all your oaths ready. Endgrains are hard to clean up as they fracture so easily. Work carefully and don't leave any unwanted holes.

Don't forget to sign your work. Get in the habit of signing all your things, even practice pieces. This is to instill pride in you, to identify the piece (who knows, you may become a famous household word), and also it gives the buyer a feeling of owning an "original." You may as well capitalize on it. It is well to sign inconspicuously, but on a visible surface.

Fig. 21. The mask is nearing completion. I used the several smaller rasps pictured. I could have used only the basic horseshoe rasp but it would have taken much longer. The poor guy looks pretty miserable caught in that vise, doesn't he?

Fig. 22. Cap'n Stormalong, Koa, 12". I have done some texturing to lend interest to the piece, but I suggest you finish yours smoothly.

FINISHING

You may have thought it was difficult to begin your first piece, and it was. But it is even more difficult to know when to quit. All sculptors should work in pairs, one to hit the other on the head when he is through. Make it as flawless and symmetrical and pleasing as you can. Then stop.

Ordinarily, we would begin sanding at this point. We are not going to sand this first piece for two reasons. We are learning the use of the basic tools of sculpturing: the chisel, the gouge and the rasp. We must learn to bring our work as close to perfection as possible without relying on the crutch of sandpaper. Sanding is a problem because everyone thinks he is an expert and almost no one is. It is a destructive act.

Fig. 23. Mask, W. S. Brown, Mahogany, 12″. Even our fuzzy friend from Fig. 20 made it (although he took a lot of sanding).

A lot more wood can come off with sandpaper, particularly around sharp detailed edges, than you can imagine. Sanding also leaves an abrasive residue on the surface of the wood that quickly dulls your fine steel gouges and rasps. Never follow sanding with rasping or chiseling. In a later chapter we will explain what you must do if this cannot be avoided. Just don't do it for now.

If you are convinced that you are otherwise done you can apply the sealer. As you know, all wood fibers are porous. An oil finish would soak in forever. A primer coat of thinned shellac, eight to ten parts of thinner to one part of white shellac, will seal these pores and keep the finishing oil on the surface. Apply the thinned shellac liberally, wipe off the excess and let it dry. This will protect the finish for now. We will apply the oil finish after another chapter or two.

Congratulations! You have successfully, I hope, completed your first piece of sculpture. Take a picture of it for your records. Jot down in a little log book the name of the piece, the type of wood, the size and date of completion. Give it a number "1." Someday you will be entering 100 or 1000 in that log. You are on the way.

Now that Number One is under your belt and you are a master craftsman, go back to the second part of Chapter One, the section called "More on Tools," and learn some more details before we try another piece.

FOUR

CREATING IN WOOD: PROS AND CONS

SCULPTURE separates itself from other art forms in two basic ways. It has three dimensions and it is irreversible. These unique qualities must be the bedrock of your attitude and approach to your work. If they aren't, then you are not doing good sculpture.

THE THIRD DIMENSION

Obviously, painting lives on a flat canvas plane, its artistic area defined by height and width. Just as obviously sculpture adds a third dimension: depth. Obviously, that is, until the new student tackles his first few pieces. When he finishes them he will almost assuredly discover that he has created a drawing on wood. His design will have height and width, but its depth will be almost non-existent. It will be a block of wood with shallow surface relief. This is natural, since most of us are attuned to the restricted canvas or flat pages of art books. We see most of our drama on the two-dimensional screens of the movie-house or the television set. Even symphony orchestras are pressed onto twelve-inch flat discs or ribbons of magnetic tape. It is little wonder that in art we don't expect to find that third dimension that we live in all day long.

Why worry about depth? Why must sculpture differ from other media in this way? Because depth is what defines sculpture. Its peculiarity is its being "round." You will have to work hard to overcome the propensity to make your pieces flat. Three techniques will help you in this.

AVOID FRONTALITY

Much bad sculpture is like wallpaper. It has but one side to be looked at. Other bad sculpture is like a coin. It has but a head and a tail. Yet more sculpture, little better, has a very limited number of sides, or façades. A good piece of sculpture should have at least a million silhouettes. One of the biggest battles of the new—or experienced—wood sculptor is the battle of frontality.

True, as you stand and study a particular piece it will seem to have only one shape, the one at which you are looking. It will remain so until you move. When you do, no matter how imperceptibly, the piece will take on a different appearance if it has been done properly. Its silhouette will change. The better the sculpture, the more you will be drawn around it to see what else there is to it. The rhythmic flow of the shifting silhouette not only pulls you around but is pleasing in itself.

I cannot describe the magical combination of shapes that will lure the viewer around the piece. The reason is simple. Form is unique. No two forms are exactly alike. You have to make the form, look at it, judge its value, and then proceed to alter it. You cannot read a book and learn about good form and bad form.

One fine way to overcome the frontal problem is to open up the wood (Fig. 24). This doesn't necessarily mean just to make a hole in it. It means to create more surface area. This will give you three times as much sculpture, good or bad. I can't guarantee the good or bad part, but the chances of an interesting piece are going to be greater if the surface is greater. Use all the wood or call it a bas-relief.

A hole isn't just a hole, by the way. Henry Moore has shown us that it can be much more than that. It is a mass of air. It is a form. While you are opening up the wood and avoiding the ogre of static frontality, don't neglect the possible use of enclosed space within the piece itself.

Fig. 24. Father and Daughter, Monkeypod, 27". Notice how opening up the wood gets the most from the design. There is no danger of frontality here. Can you feel the pull to walk around the piece?

Fig. 25. Cogs in a Gear, Ebony, Walnut and Amaranth. If one face had been completed before another was begun the meshing unity of the various forms would have been lost. Note too that we have escaped frontality again.

WORK ALL AROUND

The best way of all to avoid frontality and make your piece truly three dimensional is to work all around it. This point cannot be overstated. There are only three or four key ideas required to do good work. One of them is that you simply must work on your piece of sculpture as a beaver works on cutting down a tree. You must go around and around and around. If you concentrate on one spot it won't work with the rest later on. It won't match.

When you are done all the pieces must fit together. Nature's things fit together. Things look as they should look. They are as they should be, unless there has been an accident. A mountain fits together. Even a fissure on that mountain that is cracked and broken away will fit if you study it. This is because the basic agents of nature, erosion and gravity in this case, operate in a logical and harmonious way. Man is neither logical nor harmonious all the time, so sometimes when he makes things they don't fit together. By working all around he can minimize this danger.

Another good reason for working all around is that you keep opposite sides fresh in your mind. Let's assume you are sculpturing a head, for instance. You have worked on the left jawline from beginning to end. It is right, down to the whisker. Now you begin the other jaw. As you get into it you will tend to forget the intricacies of the first side. This technique is not only a fine reminder but it keeps you from getting into asymmetrical problems when you didn't plan on having them.

When we say work all around, we mean more than the sides. Sculpture is *three* dimensional, and it has a top and a bottom, too. Too many of us forget to think globally, even in this age of astronauts. Be sure to work all around your work, north and south as well as other ways.

The best rule to remember is to stop and look at your work often. Look it all over. Then proceed to take off the wood that is most obviously not needed.

ADD TO BY TAKING AWAY

Forms are created in modeling by adding material, increasing the mass by lumping on more clay, for example. Sculpturing is the reverse. It is important that you take away that which you don't want. Each part is relative and dependent upon its surroundings. To make highs you need lows.

This is hard to learn. To add to you have to take away. Speakers comment that they have to have hills and valleys in their speeches to maintain audience enthusiasm and highlight their main points. The slow movement in the middle of a sonata is there for a purpose. Among other

Fig. 26. Prometheus, Monkeypod, 25″. See how the thrust and strength is created as much by the removed wood as by the remaining masses. The slender waist heightens the power of the legs and the torso.

things it contrasts with and accents the faster surrounding movements. Sculpture does the same thing. It is a simple notion to discuss but very hard to put into practice.

Force yourself to learn this axiom:

Eliminate that which you don't need.

I have often told students while they were standing hopelessly mired before their effort, "But, Joe, it's obvious that you've got wood there you don't need. That's got to come out." "I know it," he invariably replies, "but I'll get it later." Later is too late. Stand back and look at your piece in progress. Frantically take off what you obviously don't need. The secret, of course, is the interpretation of "obviously." I have taken off wood that I obviously didn't need that I did need later. Of course if you don't hazard a chance you will have nothing at all.

If you want to make something high you must make something else low. Fundamentally that is such a simple problem but I would say it is the hardest problem that a person has, particularly one who works by himself. I have seen many intelligent men waste their time trying to work on a trouble spot and I tell them, "Look, you've got to go over here and make this low to make that stand out." They will mutter "Right," and a little later do the same thing. Remember that everything is relative.

OPEN END ART

Everything is relative, including my precepts. While taking wood away is vital, another vital truth about sculpturing in wood is that once it is gone, it is gone. Irreversibility is a long word that simply means you can't go home again. Once you take that obviously unnecessary wood away you can't glue it back on again. Robert Frost once wrote a poem about coming upon two paths on a winter's walk, and he knew that he could take only one. Once he started down one path he would never be able to return and try the other. Mr. Frost must have been a wood sculptor. Removed wood is like yesterday. It was there once, but it no longer exists. This is not a philosophical question but a reality: if you take the wood off it is gone forever. Two techniques will help you not to remove obviously needed material.

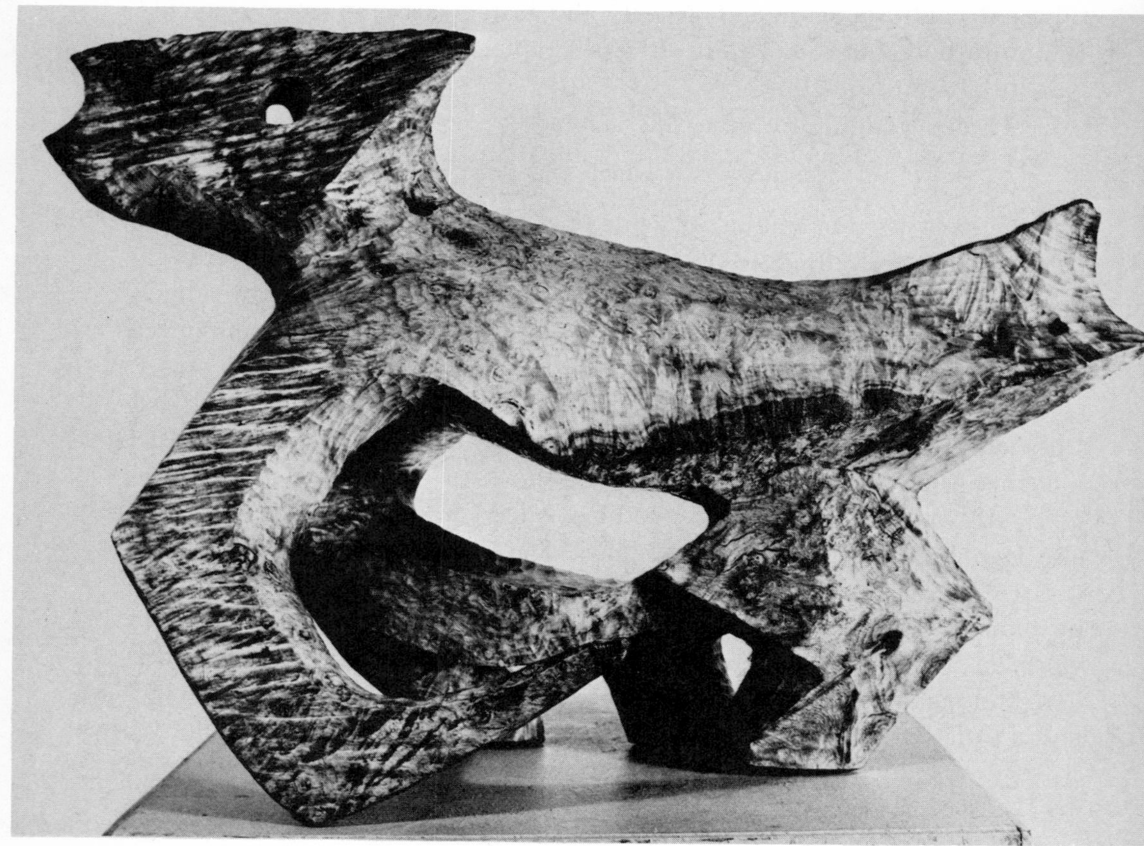

Fig. 27. Up from the Sea, Myrtlewood Burl, 20". Many of the forms of this primordial land-fish, such as the arm/fin, were born on the wood and not on paper. By proceeding slowly they were easily incorporated into the overall design.

AVOID COMMITMENT

Avoid unnecessary commitments. Make every decision a tentative one. A portrait painter is working on a head, for example, and decides fairly early that the neck should go just so. By making a firm decision and completely finishing the neck he has frozen the position and appearance of everything else on the canvas. Don't rush toward your goal too fast, particularly as a beginner. If you obviously don't need it, take it off, but remember that once it's gone, it's gone.

This is a good reason to keep away from power tools, by the way. They move through the wood so quickly that they leave you little time to observe your action and correct your next step. Sculpture is a craft of countless minor corrections. A good sculptor will make maybe a million decisions with each piece. He has to make these decisions or at the end he would still be staring at a block of wood. Make decisions, but make them of the proper magnitude. The careless student might start out briskly with great hammering and less caution because he knows what he wants to end up with and knows that he is a long way away. He is wrong on two counts.

First, he only thinks he knows what he wants to end up with. Perhaps there is a hidden flaw in the wood that will force a massive redesign. Maybe the grain is flowing in a particularly striking way but he cannot take advantage of it because he has already frozen his design. Often, and this point will be emphasized soon, he will want to change his design regardless of any trouble with the material, but it is too late.

Second, he is not utilizing all of his material if he carelessly hacks away the outer part. The only thing worse than an eight-inch block that is barely scratched is an eight-inch block that is reduced to a two-inch finished piece.

Our poor student shouldn't take the total brunt here. No matter how skillful you become with your hands and your eyes, you must always be cognizant of this potential danger. You just cannot go to the heart of the matter. True, the better you become the faster you become. Mastery of the craft reduces your margin of safety, but the margin is still there. Occasionally some may be fortunate enough to go right to the finished silhouette, but if they miss it they are ruined. One must keep adjusting to keep alive. This is a popular philosophical thesis, but it is a valid artistic one, too.

MAJOR FORMS FIRST

There is a hierarchy of Form. It is, logically, major forms, minor forms and decorative forms. The dividing lines between these categories are arbitrary, but the three divisions themselves are apparent.

Develop the major forms first (Fig. 28). Then develop the minor forms. Finally, work on the decorative forms. It is that simple, but if you elect to ignore these steps you had better get your oaths ready because you will need them. Why? For all the reasons that have previously been discussed. To keep from committing yourself prematurely you must neither take off too much wood nor freeze the design. When you decorate one place and then go on to develop the other major and minor masses, you will invariably discover that your first "finished" place is too high or too low, unhappily shaped or lacking proper rhythmic flow. Two hazards are in your way. It is terribly hard to change the character of a direct carving mass without flattening it and starting over. Second, human nature abhors repair jobs and you will be tempted to let the mismatch stand. So develop the major forms first, all of them. Then graduate to the minor. Don't start the decorative work until it is certain that minor forms are all completely adjusted and in place.

Setting in the mouth shape before the rest of the head is developed will elicit deserved criticism. "Oh, what a beautiful mouth!" And that is all. It is like the painter who is told by the tactful but unimpressed critic, "My, you've framed it so well." These compliments we don't need, or deserve, if we have followed the hierarchy of our basic elemental forms.

EASY WAYS OUT

Avenues of retreat when the above precautions are ignored are glorious in their number. Two, however, reign as the king and queen of alibis.

If our man started out too exuberantly and took away what he shouldn't have, or if he just can't get his forms to work the way he wants, then he turns to this faithful old line:

"I'm going to do it cubistically."

Sadistic teachers wait with glee for the hopelessly lost fellows who look up and murmur that line. There is nothing wrong with Cubism, but do it cubistically after you know your subject, not after you know you're lost.

The second classic is more closely allied with the finishing operation. When our poor soul gets his piece so full of gouges he can't see what he is doing, he will say:

"I'm going to leave this textured."

This is a sure giveaway, because even though you plan on texturing your piece in the most flamboyant style, you must still follow the rule of completing your major and minor forms first. That means smooth it. The form must be under control before it is patterned. Never forget that a smooth

Fig. 28. Cellist, Cherry, 29". The major forms here are the top and bottom halves of the man/cello. Minor forms include the head, upper cello lines and the arm/bow. Decorative forms are seen in the mottled texturing of the chest and base.

surface can be a texture, too. Roughness is fine if it is not a disguise for lack of technique, lack of taste, or lack of time.

EXTEND CREATIVE TIME

By delaying commitment and progressing gradually an important by-product can be enjoyed. That is the extension of the creative process. Your art will improve if you keep it open-ended, if you refuse to allow your design thoughts to stop until the last stroke of the chisel and the last swipe of the sandpaper is done. Another hard concept to master is this problem of extending creative time.

Let's take our poor beginner again. He makes a drawing of what he wants to do. Then he makes the mistake of copying it onto the wood, which is fully as bad as copying out of a magazine. His creative process is done. All that remains of his task is to slavishly hack out the preset design and try to pretend he is a machine. He is just chopping out his idea. Constantly work on this problem. Texturing, for example, can be and should be creative. The more you stretch your creative time the better artist you will be.

People who work creatively in any field have this same problem. You are interested in sculpturing because you have a creative bent, correct? It only makes sense to draw out that creative effort through as much of the performance of your craft as possible. Otherwise you are going to have periods of being bored. There is no sense in sculpturing if it bores you. Similarly, if you are bored your chances of doing meaningful sculpture are very dim indeed.

Beethoven wrote the intricate Fifth Symphony a dozen different ways before he settled on the familiar phrases we know. He wrote down an idea and worked it over thoroughly. Then he wrote down another idea. A hack doesn't do this. He feels he doesn't have to. He is right, too, as long as he is satisfied with turning out hack work.

How do you extend creative time? The best way conforms with the ways to escape frontality and premature commitment. Simply stop often and take a look at what you have. You must see where you are. Each stroke of the chisel will change the value of your piece somehow. You must be aware of this. You examine the piece and make a decision as to what you should do next. After a bit you stop and make another decision. These decisions, since they are not predestined and do not follow a

Fig. 29. The City, mixed woods, 18″. The creative process was multiplied in this piece by treating each separate building and person as a discrete and complete piece in its own right, and then creatively combining them into the entire assembly. Notice how the design has avoided frontality, relied upon working all around (top and bottom), accents height by taking away height. The necessity of avoiding early commitment is obvious.

book of rules, constitute your creative process. They also enforce your habit of working all around and avoiding commitment.

Grant you, it is not easy. It is common thinking, when working alone, that if only you were an expert you would know whether to cut this place a quarter of an inch or just what to do, but the truth is the so-called expert doesn't know. He can recognize the situation more quickly, but he can't know because everything is relative.

Forms are as relative to their surroundings as are colors. Place a red next to a green and the red will change its color value. The same thing applies to forms. Place a particular one next to other forms (and sculpture is loaded with forms) and its visual impact will change. This is where your creative ability will glow.

SUMMARY

In the first half of this chapter you are told to take off wood that is obviously not needed to assure three-dimensional sculptural forms. In the second half you are told not to be in too big a hurry to take off wood or you will commit yourself.

The paradox is not as insurmountable as it may appear. I am not telling you to take off wood with one breath and then telling you not to with the next. What I am recommending is simple, so simple to state and yet so hard to enact. You must practice your craft while being aware of the general tendency not to remove wood when it should be removed. Push yourself into defining and taking away the material you don't need. At the same time, be aware that once the wood is gone it is gone forever. When you can walk this high ridge between overcautious indecision and reckless disaster, then you will have taken a giant step toward becoming a sculptor.

FIVE

THE HEAD

THE SUBJECT

Now that you have practiced the fundamentals of sculpturing you can apply them on a new piece. The next logical step up from a mask is a head. The mask introduced you to the third dimension. Now we will round that mask out and give it full depth as well as width and height. We can continue to ignore anatomy as much as possible and concentrate instead on our sculptural skills.

This head should be somewhat formal in design. A formal, or classical, approach, if you wish, requires some amount of discipline with prescribed standards to be followed. The expected number of features resides in the expected places, and the overall design is simple and uncluttered. To accomplish these goals we will have to subject ourselves to some rigidity—to discipline.

THE MATERIAL

SELECTING THE WOOD

The choice of wood you make for this or any other piece will have a definite bearing on the outcome of your work. Several basic decisions must be made.

Shape: Obviously the shape of the wood will influence your design and attack.

Fig. 30. The Princess, Butternut, 14". The features are not Grecian but their symmetry and simplicity give this little head a classical sense.

Size: A big subject requires a big chunk of wood. Conversely, it is expensive, time-consuming and just plain wasteful to work a large piece of wood down into a small subject.

Color: Any sudden change in grain color will be interpreted by the viewer as a line, just as if you had incised it with a gouge. Also, lighter colored woods are more suitable for some subjects than dark or multi-hued woods, and vice versa.

Grain: Grain structure will have a definite bearing on the overall character of your piece. A heavy oak with its rugged grain is completely different from a fine-grained linden, for example.

Remembering these things, let's go through the mental process of selecting a proper wood for our head. For every design in mind there is an optimal piece of wood somewhere. Maybe you don't have that particular one, but if you have three or four pieces of wood around the house one of them is going to be better than the others for your purpose.

Let us imagine that we have eight or nine different chunks of wood at our disposal:

Walnut
Monkeypod
Myrtlewood burl
Kamodil
Mahogany
Teak
Linden
Butternut
Cherry

Our head is going to be symmetric in design, with the flow of the grain supporting this symmetry. It should be life-size, and its surface should be as free from mars and flaws as possible so as not to detract from the simple design.

We can immediately throw out the walnut as being too big. This chunk we have is an old log from a tree 18 inches in diameter, and I am surprised you didn't notice. The monkeypod and myrtlewood burl have violent grain coloration and configuration, so they can be dismissed for defeating the classical approach we are after. The kamodil might be flawed on the inside. After some poking around we think it is too risky to try. It will be fine for another piece, but a classical head cannot survive unexpected pockmarks and worm lines. Similarly, the mahogany's layered or overlapping grain doesn't suit our purposes exactly. The resulting pattern may be attractive, but it will also probably detract from the fine lines we are hoping for. The teak splits easily. At your stage of development I would suggest passing it up. You are going to have enough trouble as it is. The linden is a wonderful wood to work with. It is hard with no grain problems at all. Unfortunately that is its failing here. It has no grain as far as the eye can tell. The one thing we will be striving for in this piece is the symmetry of grain. We want to learn how to use grain to enhance our design. We cannot learn this without grain, so the linden is out.

This leaves the butternut and the cherry. Our particular piece of cherry is just a touch on the small side. We want our head to be about six inches in diameter at the base. Because our piece is quarter-sawed, wherein a log is cut into four equal parts with two cuts through the middle, it would mean setting the head at an angle to utilize the grain flow. If we didn't we would get distorted grain lines on our head—the sculpted head, that is. What we want is a logical, simple and beautiful flowing of the grain around the head, the grain creating the contours of the head and face. By the way, accustom yourself to working with quarter-cut wood as round logs are more difficult to find. Except for this point, the cherry would be perfect. It is a hardwood, it has character, it looks and feels right.

That leaves the butternut, and as luck would have it, it is just what we are looking for. It is a little softer than walnut, but still workable. It is light in color, but retains character. We will still have to put our design in a little cattywampus, but not nearly so skewed as in the cherry. The sapwood is strong, unlike many species whose sapwood is soft and spongy. The sapwood, by the way, is the living part of the tree where the great volumes of sap move up and down on the outside of the already dead heartwood. Our particular chunk of butternut has a little lump of sapwood, lighter in color, perched on top. We can use this as a little white cap on the back of the head.

After reviewing all these pieces you will have to make your decision. Yours was probably different from mine, because we are different people with different tastes and different skills—and different chunks of wood. Probably if I were doing this piece strictly for my own edification I would select the monkeypod because of the challenge of the more active wood. The failure chances are high, however, so we will stick with the butternut for now.

The important thing to be gained here is that you should approach the selection of wood carefully as it is a definite factor in the eventual outcome of your work of art.

LEVELING

People feel better if an object doesn't look as if it is going to tip over. There are two kinds of balance: static symmetry, where the peculiarities of one side of an object are equally matched by the same peculiarities on the other side; and dynamic counterbalance, where everything is working in different directions, but the total effect is one of balance. Sculpture, and other things for that matter, looks better if its balance is dynamic. A static piece is just what it sounds like: unmoving, stolid and dead. Sculpture, particularly sculpture depicting living things, usually attempts to capture the liveliness of its subject. There are some exceptions, but a piece that is "a little off," a little skewed, is more alive and more appealing than a machinelike perfect image.

It is much easier to end up with a balanced piece if you start out with a balanced piece. That means you will have to learn how to level the base. A neophyte might pick up a piece of wood and say, "I'll make something out of this," and plop it down on the workbench and start carving. Chances are he will never get it right because it is always going to look crooked. He will try to correct this, but it will be too late. The first thing he should have done was to balance the wood so that it could carry the design, both visually and mechanically. It doesn't have to be straight up and down, but it should be stable. This is accomplished in two stages of leveling.

First you have to know where to cut off the base. Prop the wood on a bench by sliding washers under the high spots until it stands the way you want it by itself without wobbling. Stand back and look at it and be sure that it is exactly right. Now find an object of the proper height, such as a matchbox, and while holding a pencil on top of it, draw a line around the base. Put it in a vise and cut it off. Now the base is fairly level.

To really flatten the base requires a level work surface. Rub chalk on a piece of fine sandpaper. Now place the newly cut base on the sandpaper and wiggle it a bit. File the chalky residue from the high spots on the base. Be careful here or you will only make further indentations. Repeat until the base is uniformly chalky. Now you have a very level and flat stand for your piece. If the width of the base is somewhat thick it will be almost impossible to make it completely level. In this case remove some wood in the middle of the base, leaving the perimeter untouched. Repeat the chalk routine and the piece will stand just as solidly as if the

Fig. 31. The wood has been cleaned and is ready to use. Notice how I have drawn the crown of the head at an angle to take full advantage of the grain. Also notice that the longitudinal axis is a little off center to ensure liveliness. Compare the chalk profile with Fig. 30, and you will see how much the design was changed during the execution of the piece.

middle wood were still there. Do this only when finishing a piece, because at the beginning you will not be certain just where the edge of your base will be.

SHAPING

ROUGHOUT

The first thing that must be done is to clean up the wood. On a sensitive piece such as this we must be sure that no flaws are going to surprise us as we approach the final surface. This surface business is important. Much is made of sculpture being an art of mass, but the ultimate surface appearance is extremely important also.

First clean off the obviously bad wood. There will be places around the edges that have been split or torn or even soiled. Hew them away immediately. Don't worry too much about the ultimate objective right now, but please don't carelessly carve away some good wood that may be needed later on. When the surface is relatively clean, take your scriber and pick away at any potential danger spots. Knock on the wood and begin to familiarize yourself with the finding of hidden flaws or slumps.

An experienced sculptor would actually combine this roughout stage with the preparation of the major form, but at this point it is well to separate the two functions and get a clear idea of exactly what is being done and why. Only when you are satisfied that the flaws that you know about are gone, and you can only fool yourself here, only then is it time to go on to the major form.

THE MAJOR FORM

We need as perfect a major form as we can get. All our success —or failure—is based on the proper execution of this step. Complete the major form before beginning the minor forms.

We want a beautiful rounded shape for our major form. This will represent the princess' head. All sculptural shapes, by the way, do not have to be "beautiful" or "rounded." Cap'n Stormalong, my mask in Chapter 3, is certainly neither beautiful nor rounded. For this subject, however, the two adjectives are valid. We want the shape to take advantage of the grain so that the grain lines will help to form the hairline, for example, and the forehead, eyes and cheeks later on. Remember to work all around as we have emphasized, particularly in a spherical form such as this head.

This headshape is not realistic. It is only a chunk of wood. We can establish the identity of its being a head, however, and that we must do. There are two ways to set this head into my piece of butternut.

Naturally you have a different piece of wood and therefore have different alternatives. We have to remember that the head is deeper from nose to nape of neck than it is wide from ear to ear. In the butternut the head could be seven inches high, but the grain would fight us all the way. The proportions would be wrong. It is better to turn the head a bit so that the grain will work with us. Some size is lost, but much more is gained in the overall unity of design.

All this talk about being symmetrical and using the grain is important, but you may have noticed in the figures that the head is slightly off the center of the grain. It is off just enough to make it more alive. Dynamic is the more precise, less interesting, word. Look at yourself in the mirror. Is one side of your head exactly the same as the other? No. Even in a classical head this is important. Static symmetry is dead.

A few reminders might be helpful here. While you are bringing your major form to shape, be sure not to commit yourself before you have to. Maybe you think the neck will be right HERE and it will be just THIS size. Well, fudge a bit. Something might happen to make you change your mind. If you have left a margin for error, then there will be no problem. It might not hurt to review the last chapter again before you arrive at what you think the completion of your major form is. Take your time. Take off what is obviously not needed, but don't commit yourself too soon.

We have all been brainwashed into thinking that certain human proportions are good and others bad. Anatomy is a subject that is too large for this book, and you will have to study it elsewhere. Please do be aware that working in contemporary art does not excuse you from applying the requirements of structure, human or otherwise.

We are mechanically carving here. Try to work toward the center of the mass to gain form and work with the grain. Take your time and remove small bites of wood. When rasping, curve the rasp *gradually*. You will have a tendency to flatten the rounded surfaces, so take small bites and keep rounding, rounding. Remember that nature abhors straight lines. Keep your work turning on the holder like a chicken on a spit. Do not stay too long in one place. When in doubt, shellac and rasp it out. The thinned shellac will temporarily discolor the wood and reveal the spots that need further work.

Stop and look. I don't do this enough and nobody else does it enough. Constantly redraw the centering lines. Sometimes it helps to get

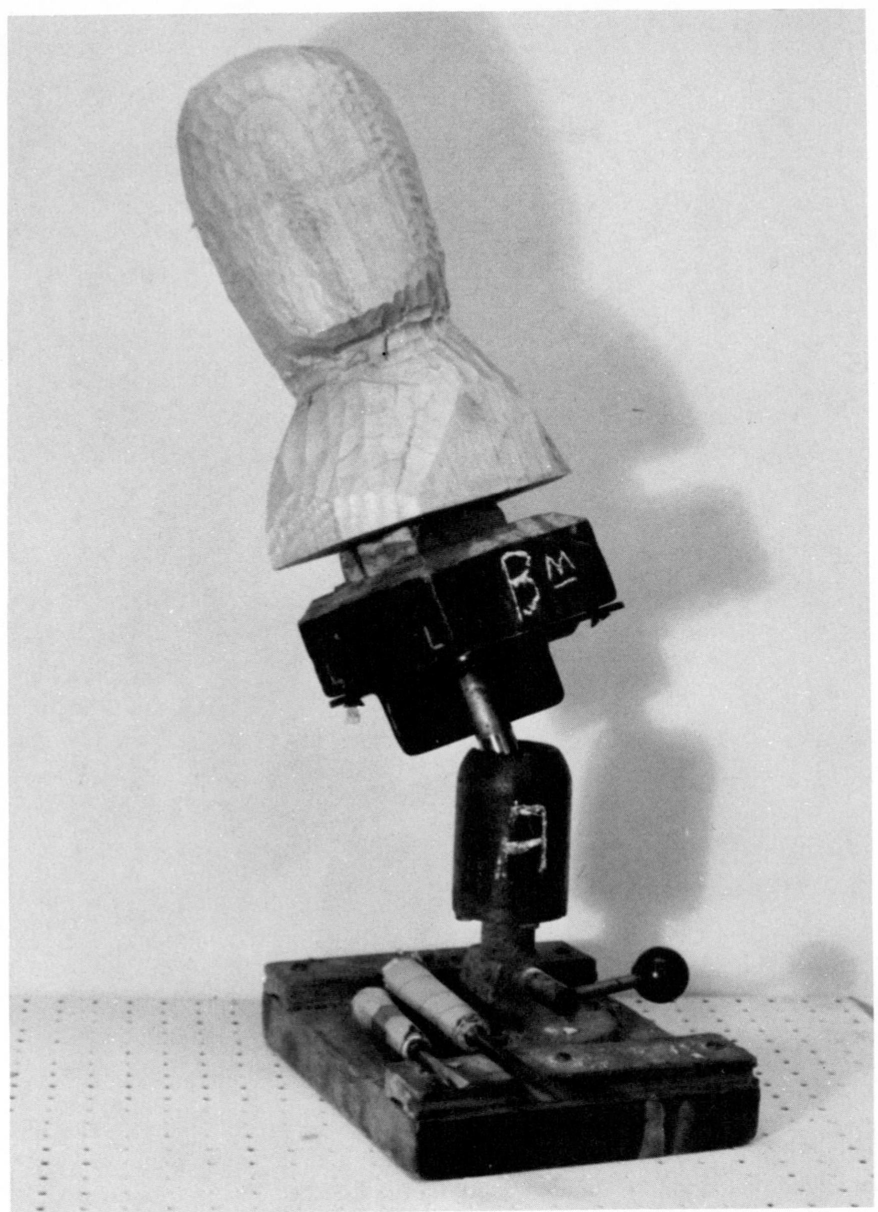

Fig. 32. The head and shoulder areas are beginning to evolve. Only the one-inch chisel and half-inch medium gouge have been used thus far. The power arm (A) makes it easy to move the work about. This view shows the fastening of the modified base (B^m) to the power arm quite clearly. Notice where I have dabbed a cross on the face with my shellac brush for quick orientation.

Fig. 33. A dark patch of untouched shellac behind the ear location pinpoints a problem area. I have obviously stayed away from it as the grain is not working properly in that spot yet. The dark place on the forehead is where excess wood is being removed to shorten the face. The beginnings of a neck are starting to appear.

a different colored background so that you can see the wood and its silhouettes better. We want all the wood we can get, so we are constantly being careful not to prematurely commit ourselves.

In my piece it is obvious that something has to be done about a hump of wood behind the right ear, or where the right ear is going to be. We have been consciously nursing this area along, and now it is time to do something about it. It has become "obvious." It has been a worry to us because our design came to the flat edge of our material here and it was our dominant limitation. Instead of worrying and toying with our problem, however, we did the right thing and went all around the rest of the headshape to bring it down to where it should be. Then, and only then, could we see what obviously had to be done about the flat spot. This is most important. Leave your trouble spots alone until you have defined the trouble spot's environment. Make the situation. Then tackle the trouble spot.

We could remove wood from the front or rear. Now that we understand the problem we make a judicial decision to remove wood from the front. We will mark the area with chalk and work toward the center of the trouble spot. It is perfectly safe because we are following the marks. We are removing material that is bothering us and the quicker that we can get it out of the way the better. We still hold only an overall headshape in mind with as few restrictive minor design notions as possible. If the overall headshape is gotten right now it will be hard to lose, and if it is wrong now it will be impossible to win.

The flat place is repaired. Since one side was nursed so much because of the other, we can now round the entire piece out. Go around the poles and go around the equator. It is fascinating how it all begins to unravel and make sense. There comes a magical time when all the hard and deliberate effort suddenly begins to come alive. It is a fine moment.

At this point the head is obviously too long. I must take a little off the head or the chin, but I did not commit myself in either area so I have excess wood at both places. Calipers may prove handy here to examine your own headshape. Eyes often deceive.

If you are temporarily lost, don't be afraid to rasp to find out where you are. Rasping should only be feared if you are neglecting the more efficient and more personalized chisel. Redraw the guidelines. Stand back and look for the next obvious spot to remove.

The headshape is still not right. We must reduce the length even more. It hurts because we thought we were done, but if we don't fix it now we will have a hatchetface, and who needs that in a classical head? An average face is roughly divided into thirds: from hairline to brow,

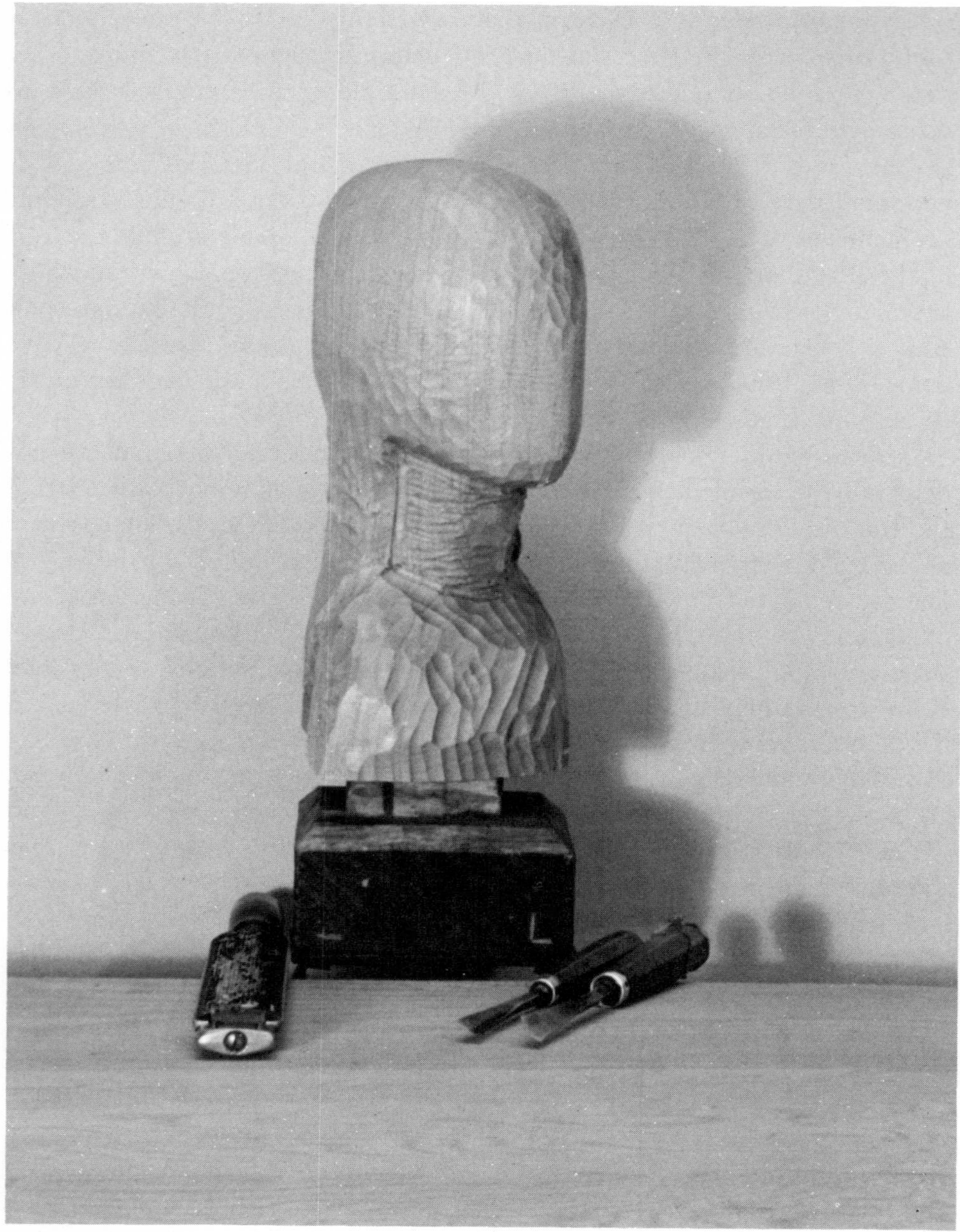

Fig. 34. The neck, jawline and hair have been further defined. The face is still too long, but there is ample wood to be removed. The rasp has revealed that the grain is going to work nicely around the face and forehead. Note the absence of features late in the shaping of the major form.

from brow to bottom of nose, and from nose to bottom of chin. Typical proportions from front to back are 2/3 from nose to ear and 1/3 from ear to back of head. There are an infinite number of variations, but we are in the identity business now so we had better keep these rough proportions in mind. If we chose to make a face all forehead—and we do know some people that appear to be all forehead—we would have a bald-headed man whether we wanted one or not.

We are ready now to do something about the major form of the neck. It is a big form, carrying all of our life support avenues from our body to our bulky head. A neck requires a lot of room. Geometrically, it is a large forward-slanting cylinder. A man's neck, in artistic shorthand, tapers up from a broad base. A woman's neck is long. Our princess, being noble, possesses an even longer neck to make her look regal. The adam's apple is squelched in female classical heads, at least in mine.

The grain, which we are concentrating on, was largely committed when we originally laid out the head in the basic block. We can vary it somewhat now, but the major commitment has already been made. As we go about the head gradually removing tool marks we suddenly reach another magical plateau where everything falls together. These moments make it all worthwhile.

Stop and look and decide what should come off next. The novice will be tempted to say, "The features—I'm ready for the features." Alas, he is premature. He probably would have trouble placing the ears. Ears are rather ugly in real life and are often done away with in artwork, but the ear-mass has to be allocated or the entire head will fail. Draw a box where it should go on either side of the head, on the same general plane as the nose. The head form, by the way, falls back quite rapidly behind the ears. The bottom of the ear coincides roughly with the chin. Chalk all this in and take a look. The center of the mouth is about 2/3 up from the chin toward the nose. I happened to edge my mouth in a little low, but I have plenty of extra wood so it will cause me no problems.

Understand that we are talking about specific features, but we are not actually creating them yet. We are merely arranging the areas in which these features will reside.

Go around again and build an aesthetically sound form. Bring the mass to a place where the head, shoulders, face, neck and eyes can logically reside. This is important, for if it is done right you probably won't go wrong, but if you do it wrong you can't go right.

AMENDING

THE MINOR FORM

Only after we have fashioned the head shape so the grain is working around the major form the way we want, only then can we proceed to the minor forms. What are these minor forms? They are amendments to the major mass. Establishing the hairline between the cranium and the face is one. The result is still one form, amended, and not two separate forms. Put in the hairline tentatively and see how it looks. Is the major form still working properly?

Bring the hairline all the way around the face. We are still not far enough down into the wood, so we are going to bring it in a little closer to its eventual depth. As you become more adept and more experienced you will be able to approach your ultimate design more quickly.

CORRECTING MISTAKES

It happens that I made a mistake at this point. I chipped the wood by going the wrong way against the grain. I hit the chisel too deep and too hard when it was in a splintering situation, and one point of the chisel dug into the wood and split it off. Experience usually allows us to move more swiftly, but we are all vulnerable to careless mistakes. I am glad it happened so that you will realize that this task is never easy. This joy was not obvious at the time of the mistake, however. What we have to do now—see how I share my error with you—is to stop and reassess the situation. Our first job is to clean out the area where the chisel went in to find out how serious our problem is. It hurts, but just as the dentist must get out all the fragments of an extracted tooth, so must we remove all of the debris or it will hurt us later on.

Rasp carefully around the offending area. It is on the right temple of the princess where the hairline is most vague. We have a gash about a half-inch long and a sixteenth-inch deep. Sounds small, doesn't it? We will see. Remember that the rasp is similar to the chisel in that if you do not rush it the cutting action is better. It has time to cut rather than tear the wood.

We are rasping a lot here because the rasp is more controllable than other tools. Douse the work area with thin shellac or Watco oil occasionally to reveal the remaining scars. It is apparent that one side of the face is now deeper than the other. This is not in our plan and we will have to correct it. There is nothing we can do about the low spot. It is there and it is ours. We will have to work on the surrounding high spots instead. Chalk an "X" on the low spot to force yourself away from it.

Since the face has been narrowed, we must shorten it to keep the proportions right. We can take off from the top or from the bottom. Luckily we still have some extra material at both ends for just this contingency. Never commit yourself until you have to. In this case the top will be better. It is misfortunes like these that make you realize how the entire piece blends into one entity; a sixteenth-inch mistake requires the reworking of the entire head.

Sometimes it seems as if you can't get the piece going again after a tragedy such as this one. I sometimes resort to something I am not proud of and I don't recommend, but you should know of all the alternatives. If I am hopelessly bogged down I reach for my biggest chisel and slash as deep a gouge as I can into the recalcitrant design, forcing myself to work with a completely different design situation. I cannot recommend it, but it works more often than not. The proper way, of course, would be to professionally work away at the stubborn piece until it is skillfully brought to rights. As a human being, however, I find that an honest slash at obstinacy satisfies more inner needs than does mere professionalism.

FEATURES

Now that the outer forms are completed and the blunder corrected, it is time to put the features in. Mark on the face with chalk or pencil where the nose and mouth and eyes will go. Just a line will suffice for now. These are not final lines, and we will be amending them continually. We can work relatively ruthlessly at first. Put in the area of the nose, mouth and eyebrows by incising small tentative lines with a veiner or small gouge. Leave lots of room, a quarter of an inch or so, for unexpected tragedies. Now you have a tentative starting place.

Start by cutting away the wood obviously not needed. Begin with the eyes, just to be arbitrary. We will have to be careful with our deep gouge here or we will be in trouble again. We know that cheeks protrude less than eyes; we know we have more wood than we need in the cheek area; therefore we take some away. We know the lower lip is almost always behind the upper lip, so we take some of that out. We are looking for the petulant look that adolescents seem to have, that look of false security and certain superiority. For the same reason we will use a closed eye connoting inscrutability, not because it is easier to carve—which it isn't—but because an adolescent is inscrutable.

My choice of butternut is an education for me, as the wood is not as hard as I thought it would be. You would do better to stay with a harder wood awhile. My chisel lags in the wood quite often, which is a signal to resharpen it. Never work with dull tools.

Fig. 35. The major form has been amended and the features are penciled in. She is certainly going to be a haughty girl.

Fig. 36. The princess ready for the final stages. The grain is working. The forms are right. The tools shown were used toward the end: deep gouges and rasps for final amending. Riffle rasps lean against the base with a few scrapers at their feet. Neither item is necessary but each makes the work go more efficiently.

Keep changing your tools so that you are using the right tool for the right job. About now you will stand back and discover that you have a face. Continue drawing guidelines so that you don't become lost. The softer the wood the harder it is to create precise lines. Stop and take a look. My princess' face is a little small, so I will have to adjust by reducing the entire headshape somewhat. After that chore I can put the features in more firmly. Set them in hard and crisp, as the finishing process will soften them somewhat.

Now we have established the identity of the head. Our head is representational in that it is the head of a young human female, but it is also abstract in that it is not a copy of adolescence but an entity in itself. We have adjusted, distorted and eliminated to make a point. There is nothing to be gained by showing the hair in her nose for me, but if you enjoy being purely realistic then you ought to be. Now we can elaborate on the design by analyzing, taking a step and analyzing again. The grain is working well and the natural design of the wood is being used to our advantage. Before we know it, we are done with this step.

DECORATIVE FORMS

The major form of the head is complete and the minor forms of the features, the hair and the neck are complete. That leaves the decorative forms. The beginner is timid at this point, and well he might be, for experience will help you here. Some think that this is when the artist leaves his trademark, but that is not true. One's style is embodied throughout a piece, especially in the major form.

At the beginning of a piece there will be a bushel of chips on the floor at the end of a day. At this stage, however, a day's work will result in a handful of residue. In other words, now is the time for caution and forethought. I occasionally get bored during this time, wanting to finish the piece and get on to the next one. If I work properly, though, I will become engrossed in the small problems and leave my boredom behind.

Examine the piece closely. We have left anatomy entirely since the head's identity has already been established. Now we want to strengthen our design if we can. It is strictly a matter of personal taste and judgment. No one knows what is correct. What you will know is what you try.

We can texture the base, if we please, or leave it alone. I elected to make the base textured to contrast with the clean and smooth lines of the face and head.

After that is completed it is just a matter of cleaning up as thoroughly as possible in preparation for the final stage. Experience will teach you not to leave holes or flaws, no matter how small, because they will make the finishing stage take forever. This is why we did not sand our mask, so as to learn the importance of really bringing a piece to its conclusion before sanding is begun.

SANDING

PRECAUTIONS

More energy is wasted and more mistakes are made in sanding than in any other phase of sculpturing. This is because we are all self-styled experts at sanding from the age of nine. We think we know how, but most of us don't.

Sanding is a finishing process. It must be carefully controlled or your piece will be quickly ruined. Wear a working glove on your weak hand that has masking tape wound around its thumb and forefinger to protect the glove and to make the paper slide more smoothly (Fig. 37).

As sanding must be controlled, never try to finish a piece without using a holding device. It is most difficult to produce a good finish when the piece is sliding all over the bench top. Like most good finishing processes, sanding is difficult and tedious even when it is done right. It is no fun, and it isn't very creative, but if it is not done properly all the good work you did previously is either masked or marred.

Let me remind you again that when I refer to "sanding" or "sandpaper" I am referring to all types of abrasive sheets. Only cloth-backed abrasive sheets should be used when pulling under pressure or on rounded surfaces. Paper backing is much cheaper, but it tears easily when it is bent.

PROCEDURE

The concept of sanding is to systematically remove the rough spots without adding new ones. It is important that you realize there is no exactly right grade of paper for a particular wood. We have no sandpaper chart in the Appendix. Woods and techniques vary infinitely and you will have to learn for yourself through experience. What you want to strive for now is how the right selection of paper feels against the wood, not the memorization of a table of numbers.

Ordinarily I scrape my pieces before sanding, but I find the butternut a little too soft to lend itself well to scraping, so we will skip that step.

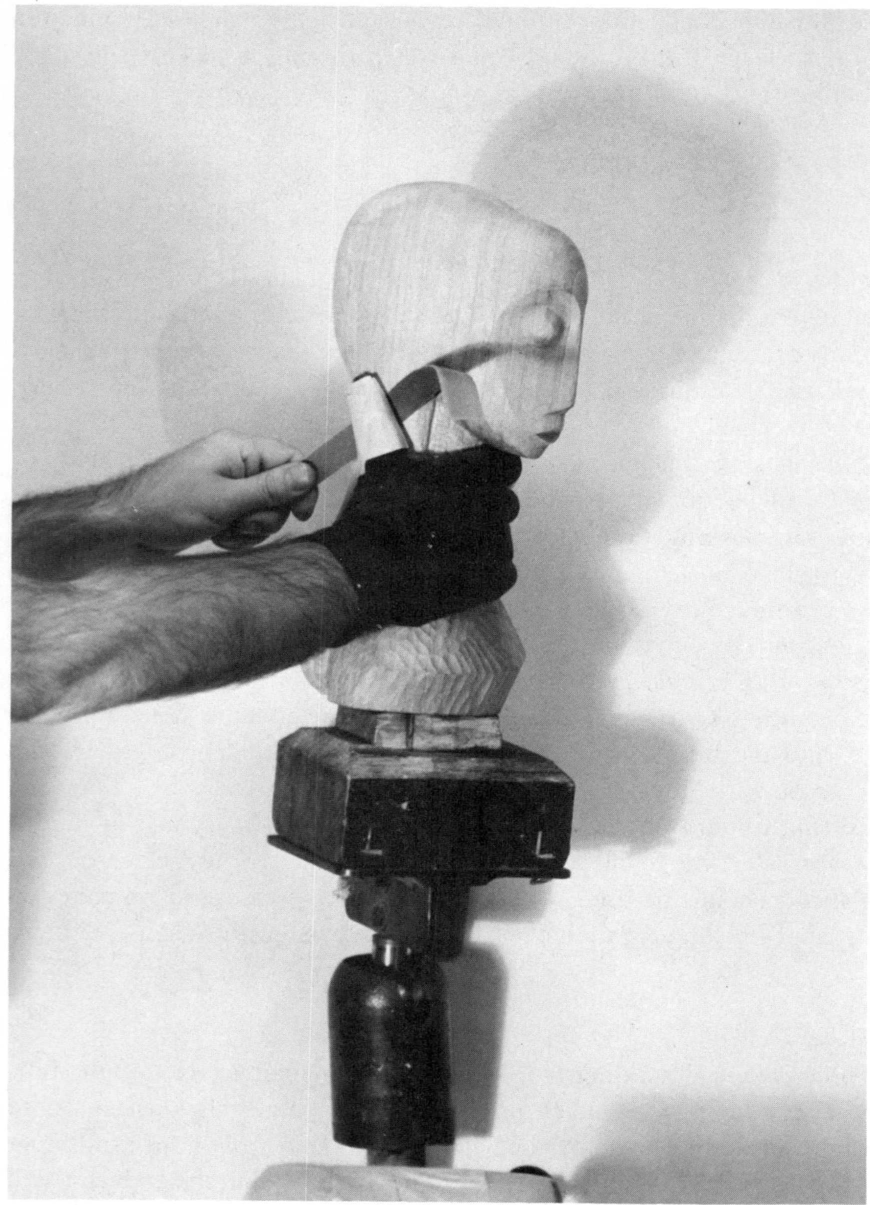

Fig. 37. Draw the strip toward you. Let your gloved hand guide the strip so that it follows the contours of the piece. This is going to tire your hands until you become used to it. Be sure not to blur the sharp lines and keep an eye on the grain.

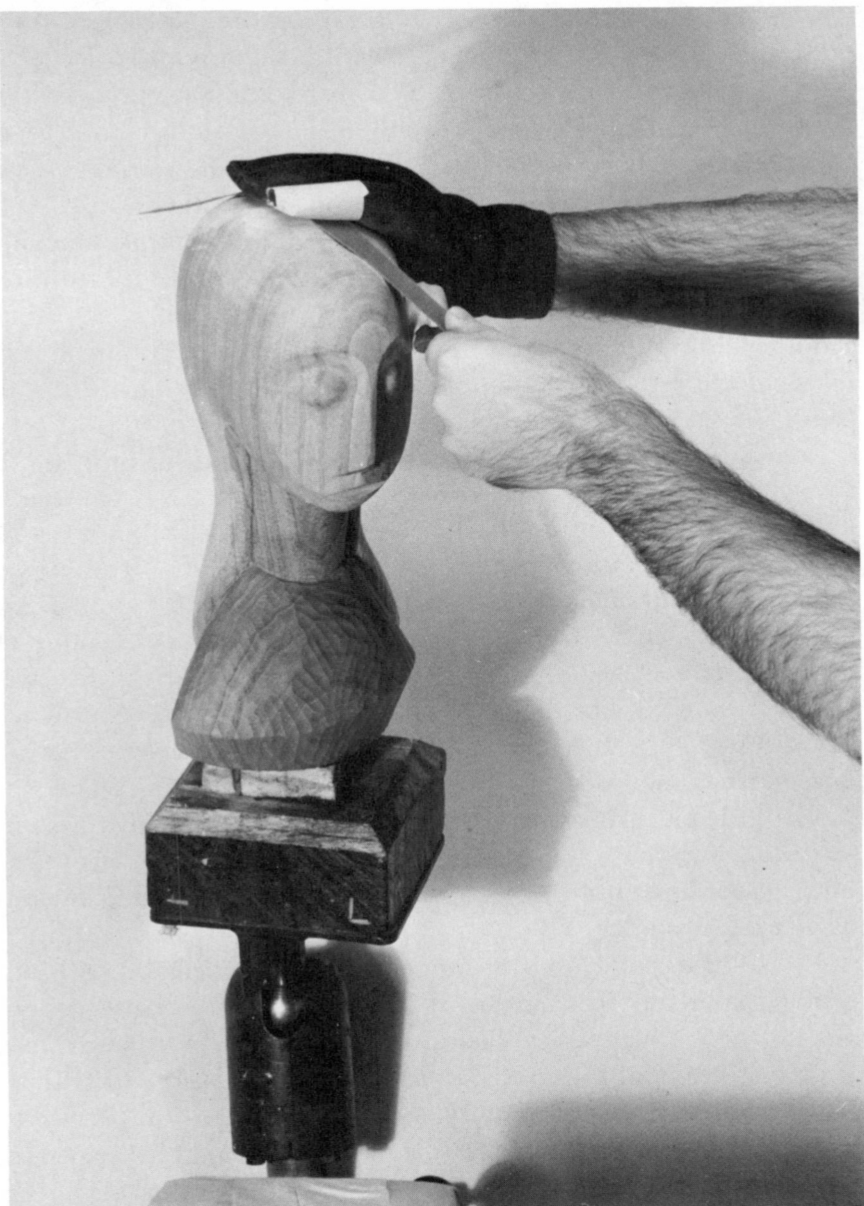

Fig. 38. Only by bearing down with the taped thumb can you efficiently smooth the surface. Work methodically and don't skip around or you will miss a place.

Start sanding with a relatively coarse grade paper. Tear it into strips vertically, against the trademark. Tearing sideways will leave puckered edges which will mar the surface. Paper-backed material will not tear evenly, so I periodically cut a supply of it and store it away. Grade 100 would be the logical starting place, but the scraping episode indicates that we had better use a finer paper, so we will start with 150.

Study the figures for the proper handling of the sandpaper. The housewife scrub-a-dub method is out. Slide the paper in the direction of the grain, if you can, particularly on flat surfaces. This is not a mandatory requirement, however, and it is often impossible to follow in tight spots and rounded areas. Just be careful. The object is to remove flaws, not make them.

Work first on the hair portion of the head, or any similar large-surfaced area on your piece. Our first grade of paper is too coarse to risk around the features of the face. Systematically work around the head and look for flaws. Remove them one by one. It is important that we make this stage a methodical search and not a random sawdust producer. We are narrowing down the bad spots, eliminating some and accepting others. It is your judgment alone that decides which flaws you can live with.

Eventually a layer of powder will obscure the work surface. Clean it off with some 2/0 steel wool and apply a coat of thin shellac or Watco oil. This darkens the wood and reveals the remaining flaws. Watco gums your tools a little more than shellac, but it is less viscous and discovers more bad spots. Review your progress and remove any remaining holes. Repeat the entire procedure until you are satisfied the surface is as smooth and flawless as you can make it.

At this point your scouring action is completed. All subsequent sanding is merely the removal of marks left by the coarse paper. Do not think that you will remove holes or flaws with finer paper. Once you lay your first grade of paper aside you should not return to it. It is now or never, so take a close inventory.

Select a finer grade paper and begin again. This paper should remove about half the ridge height left by the previous paper. I'm trying 220. The hard work is over now. It is just a matter of cleaning up your tracks. Stay alert, though, because it doesn't take much to destroy a line. Sandpaper is basically a destroyer. By now you should be able to see the beauty of the grain formed when we drew in the head on the original block

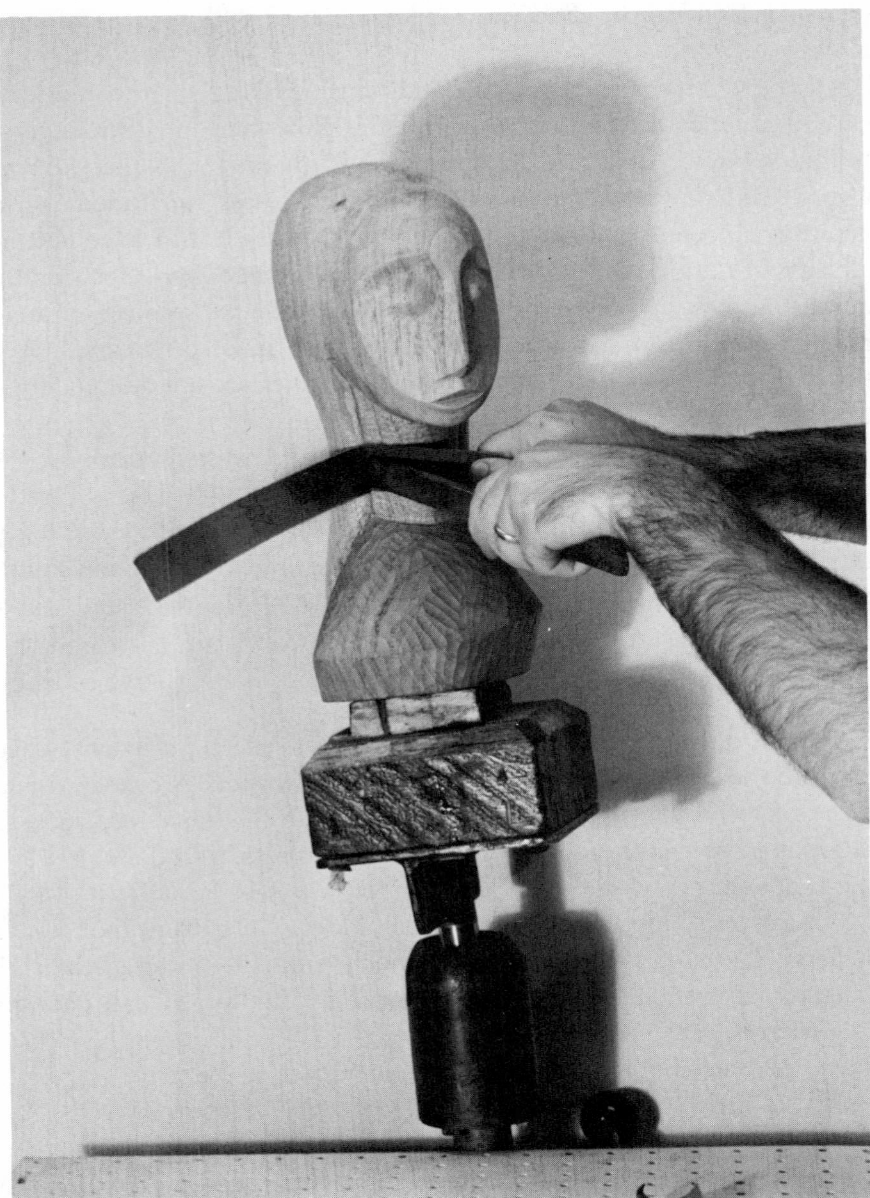

Fig. 39. Use sticks to force the strip into tight spots. As a strip fills up with debris, lay it aside and use a fresh one. These strips can be reclaimed with a brass brush which removes the shellac residue.

of wood. Good grain effect cannot be achieved with a piece of sandpaper alone.

Now take a narrow strip and start working on the face. Be most careful around the features. Take off the glove and let your fingers adjust to the surface. An errant fingernail could damage the piece now, so be aware. Pull down and away from the sharp lines for added control. Ingenuity can be applied here to get the tight spots clean. I have accumulated all sorts of odd-shaped sticks, made of polished hardwood for durability, to guide the paper where my fingers won't reach. Just because an area is unreachable doesn't mean it is unseeable. It all must be cleaned. A smooth surface should be *smooth*. Most furniture finishes are not adequately smooth to the touch of an experienced wood craftsman.

After the first paper's grooves have been systematically lowered, it is time to apply a fine grade paper. I have selected 280. This will reduce the 220 grooves nicely. This time we should try to work with the grain so that the 280 grooves (and they exist) can be disguised by the grain lines. Brush on the Watco or shellac and carefully remove all the darkened wood.

CHECKOUTS

All during the sanding operation you must guard against checkouts. These occur all too often, particularly in softer wood. A checkout is a small piece of wood that was fractured earlier and has been torn loose by the sandpaper. If it is of any size you will have to return to the chisel to amend the problem.

Never, under any circumstances, reapply a cutting tool to a sanded surface. The abrasive residue will quickly ruin the cutting edge. This applies to rasps and files, also. If you must do this to repair a checkout, the following routine must be followed.

1. Steel-wool vigorously to remove most of the grit.
2. Brush off the rest.
3. Scrape the rest.
4. Chisel carefully. Resharpen and chisel some more. Be extremely careful with the chisel here, as your design has been completed except for the alteration of the checkout.
5. File gently.
6. Follow with an old, worn-down file to clean up the regular file's marks.

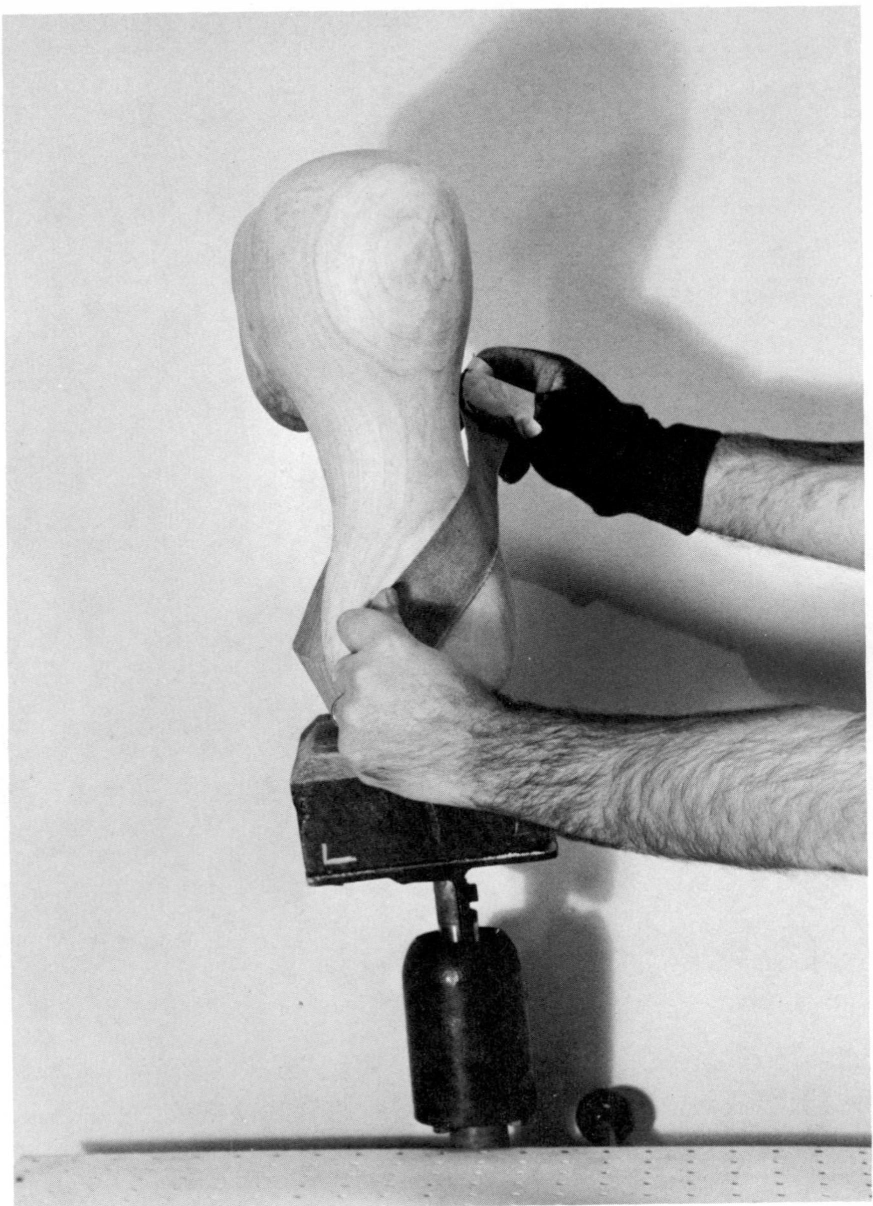

Fig. 40. The shoeshine rag approach can be used with abrasive strips in large open areas. Notice how the grain is working for us.

7. Apply thin shellac or Watco oil.
8. Resandpaper, but with caution. Remove the wetting agent, but don't go any deeper than you have to.

Fig. 41. The Princess lives. Imagine how she would have looked if the grain pattern had not been considered at the beginning. The nose and hairline around the neck save her from symmetrical stagnation.

9. Steel-wool carefully.
10. Give thanks that you escaped without destroying the piece.

Checking is a problem that is hard to avoid, especially for less-experienced sculptors. Have patience and correct those that you can and live with those that you cannot.

Knowing what you can live with is helpful. It is important not to spend forever on this finishing process. It is tedious, boresome work that takes about 10 per cent of your time, even when you are efficient. It is unbelievable how some people dawdle over this task, usually trying to accomplish with sandpaper what they should have done with chisels three stages back, and usually putting in more flaws than they are removing in the process.

THE FINAL TOUCH

Steel wool is a fine alternative on hardwoods in lieu of sandpaper. It does not leave the gritty residue that is sanding's worst feature. Steel wool doesn't work well with softwoods, however, as it leaves fine strands of metal in the pores of the wood. These later oxidize and discolor the finish. Textured areas should be steel-wooled, as sandpaper will destroy the fine lines.

Finish up with 4/0 wool. It is almost impossible to damage the finish with this as it is so fine it has primarily a polishing effect. First wet the surface with Watco or thin shellac. Let it dry for ten or fifteen minutes and then gradually remove it all. Any shellac left on the wood will mar the finish by blocking the uniform seepage of oil and leaving a mottled appearance, so take your time and get all of the shellac removed.

THE FINISH

Now stand back and take a last look. Is this what you really want? Is it the best you can do? Since perfection is elusive, you are probably not completely happy, but remember that this is only your second piece. If you are satisfied, then it is time to apply a protective finish.

If the wood is soft you will need to apply a sealer to keep the finish from endlessly seeping into the pores. The thin shellac we have been using is fine for this. Let it soak in and harden. Then carefully sand or steel-wool the fuzzy surface residue. Watco won't seal porous wood due to its low viscosity. Skip this entire step for hardwoods. We have elected to omit it with the butternut, for example.

Brush your masterpiece down thoroughly. Polish it with a lint-free cloth. Any imperfection or dirt stain will show, so get it clean now. Any good furniture polish or wax will suffice, but I have found the following preparation—used by a leading museum—to be most effective:

2 parts sunthickened linseed oil (purchased at an art supplies shop)
3 parts turpentine
3 parts vinegar

Shake often to keep the formula well-mixed while it is being applied, as it separates quickly in the bottle. Only mix a small quantity that will be used up within six months, as it tends to discolor after that.

Apply it liberally to the piece.

Let it soak in for one hour.

Wipe off ALL the excess. If you don't it will become sticky (in which case a reapplication will loosen it and you can redry the piece).

After nearly forty years of experience I have found this to be absolutely the best finish of all. As time passes and the sculpture dries, its owner can reapply the same finish.

You are done! Don't forget to enter in your logbook the completion of another piece. You also might want to go back to your mask and finish it up, after dusting it, of course.

SIX

COMMUNICATION

An argument, ancient and alive at the same time, questions whether the artist should try to communicate. Undoubtedly the caveman's friends nagged him when he was painting the animals on the wall: "Why do you do it? What does it accomplish? Are you trying to tell me something or are you just enjoying yourself?" The argument remains unresolved. We have no definitive answer for you, because there is none. Some artists, talented and renowned, have isolated themselves from their world and produced their own solace. Others, equally talented and renowned, have constantly kept a weather eye on the public, worked for onerous commissions with distasteful restrictions, and still produced masterpieces we find in all the art history books. There is no pat answer.

If you will forgive a very personal slant on this question, I would like to share my opinions with you. They may not be correct, but they are mine. I am a communicator. I believe that an artist, be he writer, composer, painter or sculptor, is a communicator. I think communication is what art is about.

Life has become so specialized that it is most difficult to communicate. To my mind this is where art can excel. We, as artists, can express common feelings, common patterns of comfort or distress, in the relatively uncluttered and unspecialized language of visual form that can be comprehended by most people of our culture. We should exercise this ability.

Fig. 42. The Hive Section: Homo Sapiens, mixed woods, 5′ 8″. We all tend to be isolated animals. The only way that man can prevail is through communication.

COMMUNICATION IN

READING

One of the best ways to learn is to read. Man prevails because he reads. A sculptor need not read just sculpturing books, just art books or just cultural books. Read anything. Read everything.

The creative process is slithery and hard to tie down. It is amazingly constant, however, no matter what the medium. Creating is the same, no matter who you are or what you work with. All truly creative people seem to experience the same routine regimen, share the same problems and evolve the same systematic solutions. There is a definite cross-proliferation of the arts that should be nurtured, particularly by the young artist. If I were pressed to name those books most influential to my craft, for example, they would include Michelangelo's letters, Pablo Casals on the creative act of performing, Agnes DeMille on the dance, and Mozart's letters.

Reading has molded my thinking and my style, albeit slowly. I am not so foolish as to think that no one before me has had a decent thought, and I am not too proud to go looking for a few of them on the bookshelf.

PICTURE MORGUE

A good way to acquaint yourself with your environment is by collecting pictures, pictures of all sorts. Newspapers call such collections a morgue. It is a repository for any item that may be useful at a later time. It can stimulate creativity by triggering ideas and reinforce techniques by establishing identities. Another reason for the morgue is that young sculptors can rarely afford to hire live models. Pictures of the human figure are motionless, too, and can be studied for days and years without the pose being dropped.

When I was beginning I used to clip pictures of everything from everywhere. I don't refer to the morgue as often as I once did, as one tends to use exterior aids less as he gains in experience. Without those aids the experience would have come much more slowly.

OBSERVATION

We are unobservant. I am, and I imagine you are, too. You may think that you are observant, but look around the room right now and see if there isn't something of interest that you had missed before. An excellent means for expanding our understanding is through the conscious use of observation.

JOURNALS

Some artists have good success with notebooks or diaries in which impressions or ideas are written down from time to time for later reference. I have tried to maintain and use these notebooks with little avail, but it is something that you should explore.

I am very good at unintelligible notes, however. I always have pencil and paper at hand with which I can scribble impetuously rushed notes that are indecipherable to all but myself. This is an invaluable aid for all but the most egotistical artist who thinks that *all* his notes should eventually be collected for a coffee table Christmas gift. I don't. I think the sculpture is the thing that should sit on the table, not the sculptor's jottings.

ANATOMY

A person making a speech has to know more about his subject than what comes out of his mouth. He needs to know more about his subject than what appears on the surface. He needs to know more about his subject than his audience. In short, he needs to know the anatomy of his subject, so that what he says will dress his subject in a lucid gown of truth rather than a shadowy disguise. A carpenter needs to know the complete anatomy of a house in order to build it, from the type of gable to the type of foundation. The same applies in sculpture. It is necessary that a sculptor study the elements of human anatomy.

This book is not going to teach you anatomy, human or otherwise. It is too vast a subject. I suggest that you enroll in a formal anatomy class of some sort. Here you have the advantage of a live model, the expertise of an experienced teacher, and the formal discipline of having to do required work within a specific time. Sign up today.

No one anatomy book is adequate. There are many anatomy books, and several of them are good, but no one book can give you all that you need to know. The subject is too vast.

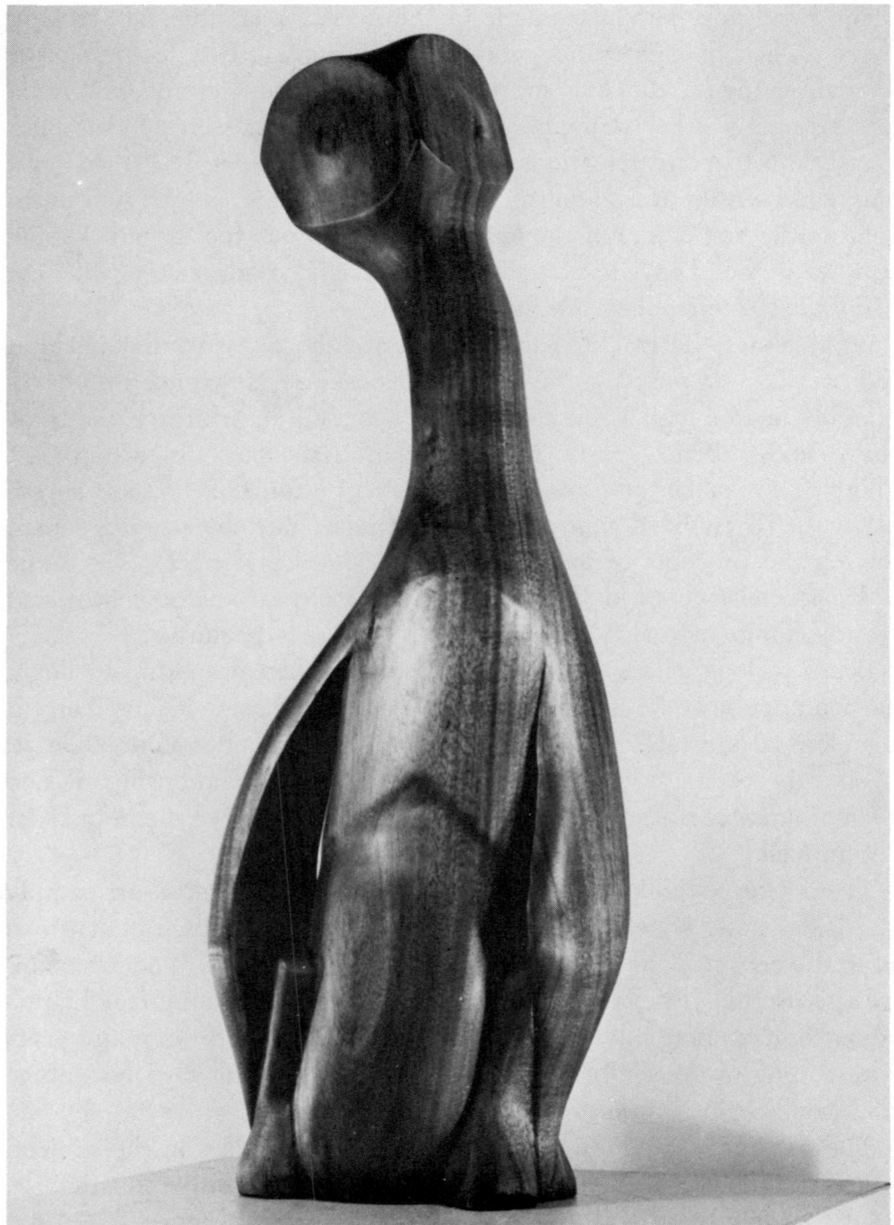

Fig. 43. Young Phoenix, Koa, 28". Anatomy even helps to establish the identity of mythical animals such as the Phoenix. The size of his head, along with his droopy wings and pudgy belly, all indicate a very young fable stands before us.

The hand is a perfect example of the need for anatomical wisdom, by the way. The body part understood least by most artists, beginners or professionals, is the hand. There are more bad hand painters and bad hand sculptors than any other definable category. Turn a person's hand palm up and ask him to point to where the base knuckle is. He has lived with this same hand within arm's length of his eyes all his life, yet he will probably point to the first crease of the fingers, about an inch too far out. People draw this way, too. They do not observe. This is a vivid example of how people do not see what they are looking at.

What about the primitives? They ignore the laws of anatomy and yet their work is supposed to be valid. The premise is wrong. Primitives are definitely anatomical. They have simply selected an arbitrary anatomy. They have said, subconsciously, that the head is the most important part of the body. They make their heads large, perhaps a third of the total length of the figure. To civilized man this appears false, but the primitive man is following the precepts of anatomy that his culture respects. The same civilized man constructs a doll for his child that has an anatomy idealized beyond any found in reality. Which culture, then, is primitive?

Learn to look at a subject from all sides. When preparing to begin on a particular subject, be it a human model or otherwise, it is most helpful to get a camera and take pictures of it from several angles—four at least. Then you can see the interplay of anatomy and the relationship of one form to another. A sculptor must see these things, and believe them, in order to function well.

There are several anatomical study aids available at art supply houses. Plaster casts of features, such as noses, ears and lips, might prove helpful to the new student, if they don't utterly confuse him. Wooden manikins are also useful a little later on. The best approach to gaining true knowledge about human anatomy is still the live model. I wasted too many years at the beginning of my sculptural career because I did not take advantage of formal training in anatomy.

The Appendix includes a list of recommended books on the subject. It is merely a guide and not meant to be all-inclusive. The important thing is not to let anatomy scare you. It is not a simple subject to master, but it is one that can be systematically learned. It demands time, effort and interest, just like any other discipline. The human body is a vital and expressive theme for any artist to explore. Some feel that it is the only worthy subject, but I do not concur. Our world harbors too many interests to allow that

Fig. 44. Cellist, Cherry, 29". This is the back of Fig. 28. Not only does it have to blend and support the front side, but it has to be just as sculpturally sound.

statement to stand. To ignore the human form out of fear or ignorance, however, would be just as limiting as dealing exclusively with it. Make up your mind that anatomy classes are in order, and begin now.

COMMUNICATION OUT

Communication implies a multilateral action. It is not a one-way street. A communicating artist cannot absorb without replying, and vice versa. Treatises have been written arguing about this and schools of art have become polarized over this. I don't care what anyone says (which is in itself an interesting comment about communication), it seems to me that a good artist *does* (consciously or otherwise) communicate outwardly what he has learned, felt and experienced.

What about the hermit who sits in his cave and draws buffalo, or a man like Gauguin who destroyed his life for the sake of creating his art, or his friend Van Gogh who never sold a painting during his lifetime? They had no apparent audience. Were they communicating? Yes, they were. The fame of an artist is unimportant: if he affects neither the emotions nor the thoughts of another person, either through direct viewing of his work or through study, then he is not a valid artist.

A communicating sculptor needs to learn his technical vocabulary and how to apply it to his craft in his own unique style.

VOCABULARY

Every field has its own vocabulary. An oil rigger and a computer programmer have their own vocabularies. They would have difficulty in conversing with one another in their working tongues. The sculptor has a vocabulary, too, even though it is a small one. Every sculptural student should learn these words and their meanings. There are only fifteen:

Form	Texture	Design
Mass	Color	Proportion
Line	Rhythm	Silhouette
Plane	Tension	Identity
Space	Balance	Symbols

Form: There is an infinite variety of forms. There are round forms, square ones, octagonal, triangular and rhomboidal forms. The variations are endless. A form is simply a shape—any shape. Some forms are more pleasing than others. Some are stronger than others. Most forms blend more successfully with certain other types of forms. Because of this variety it is

Fig. 45. In the Beginning, Myrtlewood Burl, 36″. This piece consists of several different forms, ranging from the interior spheres to the irregularly defined outer planes.

Fig. 46. In the Beginning, Myrtlewood Burl, 36″. Another view of the previous figure clearly demonstrates our point about lines. The circular line around the inner sphere is a strong feature of the overall design, even though it literally does not exist, but is a meeting place between two other forms. A strong design line also appears to run from the upper right (remembering the previous figure) to the lower left.

Fig. 47. In the Beginning, Myrtlewood Burl, 36". Another view of the previous two figures shows the role that space plays in the piece. The various textural values are obvious, but the rhythmic flow that draws the viewer around the piece can only be appreciated on the spot.

impossible to set forth rules about these combinations. Just be advised that forms take on interest and added strength in various combinations with one another. Always look for these relationships and remember them for future use.

Mass: Mass is what makes sculpture. It is the three-dimensional bulk on which the forms reside. A sculptor obviously must be aware of the effect of the masses upon each other and upon the overall design. Sculptural forms take on different characteristics than form in drawing because of the continuously flowing masses.

Line: There are many ways to make a line. The most common way for a sculptor to make a line is by joining two forms. This is where the beginner gets into trouble. It is hard to make a meaningful line by scratching a groove on a flat surface. Join some forms together instead. That makes a very definite line. A painter's line is usually formed by joining two or more colors, not by drawing a black trail of paint. It is not the line itself, but the juxtaposition of the values on either side of the line that creates interest. The cleavage of a robust young woman in a low-cut gown draws interest, not for itself but for the forms that surround it. Think of a sculptural line in this manner. It does not exist for itself, but for its surroundings.

Imaginary lines also exist. They are the lines of design present in the eye only, forced there by design insinuation. They are a part of your piece whether you like it or not and they will affect its appearance as surely as a chisel mark. Be aware of unwanted lines, imaginary or real.

Plane: This is the same configuration you learned about back in geometry class: a two-dimensional flat surface. A plane can be overt, as on the face of an outer mass, or it can be hidden or even implied in the design concept. Planes greatly affect the workings of a piece and should be handled with care, particularly if they are implied.

Space: This splendid attribute has been restored to our vocabulary by Henry Moore. It is just as massive a medium as wood. Space is real and it copies life, so try not to neglect it.

Texture: All surfaces are textured. Smoothness is as textural a quality as any, and just as difficult to produce. Students and inferior sculptors often forget the dynamic force of properly textured surfaces, just as inferior musicians seldom play loudly or softly.

Color: Grain color is a vital part of any wood sculpture. It is the essential difference between wood and other materials. Handled properly, variations in color within a piece will strongly complement a piece's design.

Overall color will affect the tone of a piece also. As you work more with wood you will come to cherish wood coloration, as it is the exquisite and exclusive attribute of wood. Applying color to wood is discussed in Chapter Nine.

Rhythm: Sculpture is like music: without rhythm it won't work. A rhythmic piece doesn't have to be rounded, but it does have to flow. Even a straight line can have rhythm if it leads the viewer's attention to other dimensions of the work. The viewer's eyes must be drawn over the piece in a pattern preconceived by the artist. If someone gawks with a stony stare at your piece, either he is dead or the piece is. Pray for the former. If the eye does not move, the piece is not successful. Rhythm is in the movement of the eye. Remember that, and always keep this movement in mind as you are designing and perfecting the piece.

Tension: One way of achieving a rhythmic flow is to build tension into the design. The various masses should be pulling together and apart at the same time. There should be a feeling of potential movement within the piece, and this can only be derived by creating a feeling of tension within the piece. A square block of wood has no intrinsic tension. A well-designed and well-sculptured block has plenty. Grain development can often be used to build this tension.

Balance: The necessities of balance, both static and dynamic, are discussed more fully in the next chapter. It suffices here to point out that all good pieces need to appear balanced, but they need to achieve this effect while still maintaining tension and rhythm. Dynamic balance is what we want, not mirror imagery.

Design: There has to be an overall design to a good piece. The putting together of all these forms and masses, lines and planes, into a meaningful work of art can only be done through a calculated and effective design. An exquisitely created hand cannot be effective if it is attached to a poorly designed arm.

Proportion: The way that these lines and planes are drawn together is seen in their proportion, one to the other. Some proportions tend to be more pleasant than others. We all learned about the golden mean in school, for example. A tiny head on a huge body will look out of proportion to reality, unless you had purposely designed it that way for effect. Proportion is the application of our principle of tying everything together within our design. No one mass stands alone and removed from another. They all relate; they are in proportion, one to the other, successfully or otherwise.

Silhouette: We spent some time on this in Chapter Four. A sculpture has a million silhouettes, if it is good, and each one must be valid.

Identity and *Symbols* are discussed later in this chapter.

Summary: You may have noticed that size is not a part of our vocabulary. I personally find no intrinsic value in bigness or smallness although some of my contemporaries do. Size seems more appropriate as an adjective, such as referring to a big form or a small rhythm.

That is the extent of the sculptor's vocabulary. He doesn't have many words to work with so it behooves him to know well those that he has. If he can master these he will grasp the essence of sculpturing. Perhaps that sounds pedantic and over-simplified, but it is surprising how many so-called sculptors do not comprehend form, or line, or rhythm. Please don't be one of them.

RULES

Now that we know the vocabulary, how do we apply it to our work? What are the syntactical rules? The sad story is that there are no real rules. That is what makes sculpturing an art. I didn't understand this when I started out, and I quickly became burdened down with some arbitrary rules that I had read once in a bad book or had deduced once from bad judgment. As an example, I was taught that if you ever showed one foot in a piece you had to show the other. That is a silly rule and it encumbered my design work for much too long.

Many students bemoan the fact that there seem to be no rules today. The truth is that there never were any rules, at least not for the true artist. He must develop his own set of tentative rules, or standards. I have no absolute rules. I certainly have a flock of tentative ones, though. When I finish a piece I go over it with my tentative rules in mind. If I discover something new that works, I modify my rules. You should learn to work with your own set of tentative rules.

Some artists today appear to have no standards at all, not even tentative ones. Sometimes this apparent lack of control is really our own ignorance as an audience. James Joyce, for example, had standards which I did not understand and so I thought his work was simply chaotic. I have since had guidance on his artistic standards and I can more readily accept his work. Other lesser artists are merely haphazard, however. Ignore them.

Rules, then, are made to be broken. Papa Haydn used to chastise his

Fig. 48. Don Quixote, Rosewood and Walnut Burl, 28". This seems to me to be a direct symbol of the old knight, but I can see why many would not respond to the conquistadore's hat at all. For them this would have to be a non-objective work.

experimenting young pupil, Beethoven. "When you become famous you can break the rules, but first you must learn them." This does not conflict with our point. Haydn wanted to be sure that his charge had a starting

Fig. 49. The Dancer, Peruvian Mahogany, 3′ 5″. Most people can accept this as a female dancer because of the symbolic hints we have used to establish identity, even though each symbol by itself is quite abstract.

point. That is what we are trying to do with you here. We do agree with Papa Haydn that eventually you must begin to develop your own rationale about what works well and what does not. It may be valid only for you, but if you do not constantly test and explore hand-me-down rules for yourself, they will be artificially binding and will murder any chance for honest self-expression.

IDENTITY

If we are to communicate directly with our audience, we should be able to establish the identity of the subject. We can do this through the judicious use of symbols. The value of these symbols in establishing identity varies with the mode selected.

Mode: An artist's presentation can run the spectrum from almost absolute realism at one end to complete non-objectivity at the other. All the space in between is occupied by representational (or abstract) art. A good craftsman can approach realism closely, but his product is still abstract (or representational) to a degree, depending upon his skill. There is no dividing line between representational and abstract modes. To abstract is to take from, which in a sense is representational. Many would consider a particular abstraction to be non-objective. Others would think it representational. To no one would it be realistic.

I rarely do a non-objective piece in my mind's-eye, but it might appear so to others who are not privy to the vagaries of my mind and emotions during the execution of the piece.

My particular artistic goal, which should not necessarily be yours, is to use the entire spectrum, from near-realism to sheer non-objectivity. It is all valid and if you shun any of these modes you are limiting yourself as surely as if you limited your use of hand tools. Most artists tend to become more abstract as time passes, but it does seem wasteful to throw away all the old tools just because a new one has been found. Successful work often seems to combine parts of non-objective, abstract and realistic modes.

Symbols: As a communicator I should know what subject I am attempting to unwrap from the wood. When working representationally I must establish the identity of the piece. Sometimes this forces an aesthetic hardship upon me, but sacrifice I must. I occasionally worry that I am still trying too hard to identify my subjects at the risk of artistic damage. Nevertheless I still consciously utilize symbols to give my viewer an inkling of what I have in mind.

The head of our little princess in the last chapter is a symbol. It represents a human female head to most people, but it is certainly not an exact duplication of a human female head. It is an entity in itself. The Greeks felt that an art work was not just a copy of life but contained a spirit of its own. We don't claim that our chunk of butternut harbors a soul but we have arranged it so that it looks as if it just might, and if it does it is definitely the soul of a princess.

A poet might describe a brook as "babbling" instead of being four feet wide by one foot deep with a gradient of twenty degrees over glacial conglomerate. He adds, adjusts, distorts and eliminates to better develop his concept of the brook. It still must elicit the image of "brook," but it needn't be scientifically classified in order to describe his concept. Art enfolds reality with symbolic paraphrasing. Ambiguity is fine if the artist is not being ambiguous with himself. If he is ambiguous by accident, that is bad. I sometimes feel that Picasso is a juggler standing with his back to the public and juggling eight cups and two saucers with one hand. He knows exactly what he is doing but he doesn't let the public in on it. As long as he knows, and he doesn't drop any cups, I believe that it is his prerogative to do so. That is the only constraint that I would make about ambiguity: in the piece, yes; in the mind, no. The only catch is that if he uses his own private symbols he cannot expect the public to comprehend them. He therefore cannot be unhappy and claim that he is misunderstood. He cannot have both worlds.

STYLE

The way that you apply symbols and establish the subject's identity will help define your own individual style. Other factors affect it also, such as theme and influence.

Theme: If we are going to communicate, what should the message be? How important is the theme to the work? How obvious should the subject be?

A danger in art today, in my opinion, is that too many people are entertaining themselves with their own work. There is a hazard in this going off and leaving the public. Art is here to serve man and man is not here to serve art. When the visual artist thinks the public should understand his message, no matter how obscure, he is making a mistake. He might better use themes that people can relate to, unless he prefers to retreat to his little cubicle and amuse himself, in which case he cannot expect his audience to be equally amused.

You have to be careful not to overextend your idea if you are creating art to be looked at by others. You can't always stand by its side and explain your intentions. I don't mind explaining a piece to someone if I am asked, but the meaning of the piece should rely on visual intimation rather than verbal explanation.

Titles are a nuisance but they should be used. Often they can sharpen the focus of your theme. "Abstract 12" means nothing except that the artist is a little pretentious. It is better to tie the piece to the real world. Sometimes I name my pieces after they are finished, particularly the non-objective ones. I don't think such labeling after the fact is cheating. It ties the piece to something with which the viewer can relate, after which he can go ahead and enjoy it for its aesthetic appeal.

Try not to fret if theme and style seem to become cluttered with fussy clichés at times. Decorative forms have their place. Michelangelo once wrote a letter to Giorgio Vasari when he was working on the Sistine Chapel, describing the progress of the great tableaux of God and man. He closed his description with, "The remainder is filled with angels, cherubim and other decorative forms which are the fashion of the time." If he can do it, so can we.

Influence: Many artists worry about reading advice like Michelangelo's. They worry about studying other art works, or even talking about their own work. Their integrity is shaken. They fear that any undue exposure to other artists will cause them to cheat subconsciously and copy the ideas and techniques of others. If you are just carving wood for fun or for instruction you can go right ahead and copy all you want. You won't hurt anything, but of course you won't produce much of value either. The opposite tack is just as fatuous. If you think that you can manufacture all of your artistic ideas yourself because you are "gifted" or because you don't want to be sullied by foreign influence, you are kidding only yourself. Even Proust, who wrote lengthy books while lying abed in a cork-lined room, drew from the unwalled experience of his youth for his writings. We talk, think and act upon what has happened to us. Most of us are not walking encyclopedias and none of us arrived in the art world on a sea-shell in full bloom as did Aphrodite. Good sculptors are learners who are always learning.

Can you shut your pristine artist's heart away from the television

Fig. 50. The Couple, Cherry, 23″. Henry Moore has done this sort of theme quite often. I was influenced by his approach to the problem, but the solution is mine, not his.

show you saw last night? Are you completely removed from today's newspaper headlines? Do you not converse with others and read new books in the hope of learning something new? You cannot isolate yourself from your surroundings, and that is that. You are bombarded all day long and even in your sleep by the ideas of others. Your ideas are not purely your own. If they were you would be drawing lines with a stick on a cave wall. Be human and be thankful that you are trainable. The best solution is to expose yourself to as much as possible. Study the methods of other sculptors. Collect pictures and discuss your thoughts with other students.

This is not copying. We all copy in the sense of employing a detail of a solution to a similar problem that we may have seen years ago at some forgotten time. It is like a pebble caught behind a rock in a stream bed. As time passes, the pebble works its way into the stream bed and eventually wears a smoothed pothole in the bedrock. Similar impressions are worn into our brains from the apparently harmless studying of others' works in the past. They whirl around and around in our heads until one day they seem to become our own idea, removed from their source. Then we can use them freely, but not until they have worn themselves into our conscience and we can accept them as our own ideas.

SUMMARY

To communicate well requires honesty. This is especially true for the beginning student. He must be honest: honest with his craft, honest with his theme and honest with his material. He can only be honest with a subject that he knows. Rodin's remarks on the truth of material apply here. Many contemporary metal sculptors treat their medium like dripping wax. Plastic work abounds that boasts bronze-like veneer. These antics cheapen the craft. Be honest. If you work in wood, be a wood sculptor.

Finally, do not be afraid of being influenced. Cross-fertilization is the only way in which we can enrich ourselves. Otherwise we are like the fruit fly that must begin again with each new generation. Don't worry about the sanctity of your style. It will protect itself. What the artist says through his style is more important than the style itself. Rote copying is animal, but synthesizing, ingesting and reapplying is human. Don't be afraid to be human. After all, Shakespeare stole all of his story lines, but just look at his results.

SEVEN

THE FIGURE

THE next logical step into the intricacies of sculpturing, after the mask and head, is the full figure. Most of the basic techniques have been explained, and now we will reinforce them through practice. A few points from the last chapter need reinforcing, too, and we will do this by following three different figures in progress. The problems of design are explored with the first, "Mother and Child." The second, "Earth Mother," will touch on anatomy and mode. The third, "Dancer," will trace the steps taken and a few of the problems overcome between the clean-up and finish of a typical figure.

MOTHER AND CHILD

The design of this piece (Fig. 56) is interesting because it developed slowly and with difficulty. I began with an attractive wood, monkeypod, that I had arbitrarily decided to work on next. I also decided, with a little help from the shape and size of the wood (Fig. 51), that my theme would be one that I have often used, a Mother and Child.

Since the material and the theme were so easily selected, you would think the design would come quickly. So did I, but it happened that on this particular day I was without inspiration. Not being a believer in the bolt-out-of-the-blue philosophy, I decided to try to grind out a good design anyway. I wanted to try something a little different than I had done before, but I wasn't sure what it was.

Before I had reached this tortuous morning I had already cleaned up the wood as we have described in previous chapters. I then took a large

Fig. 51. Mother and Child started from this handsome piece of monkeypod. The various flaws that will need removal have been circled with chalk.

piece of brown butcher paper and spread it out on a worktable. I put the prepared wood on the paper and drew a heavy line around it. This is a logical beginning, don't you think?

As we have mentioned earlier, sculptural drawing should be loose and shun details at this stage. I made ten quite different drawings on a pad over a three-hour period before I thought I had found something of merit. I tried various groupings, none of them any good. I hit upon a cradle idea, one that I had not used before. At first it was awkward, but putting the mother on her side and allowing the child to become cradled by her seemed to work. After several variations I found what I wanted, a new idea on an uncreative day. So much for inspiration!

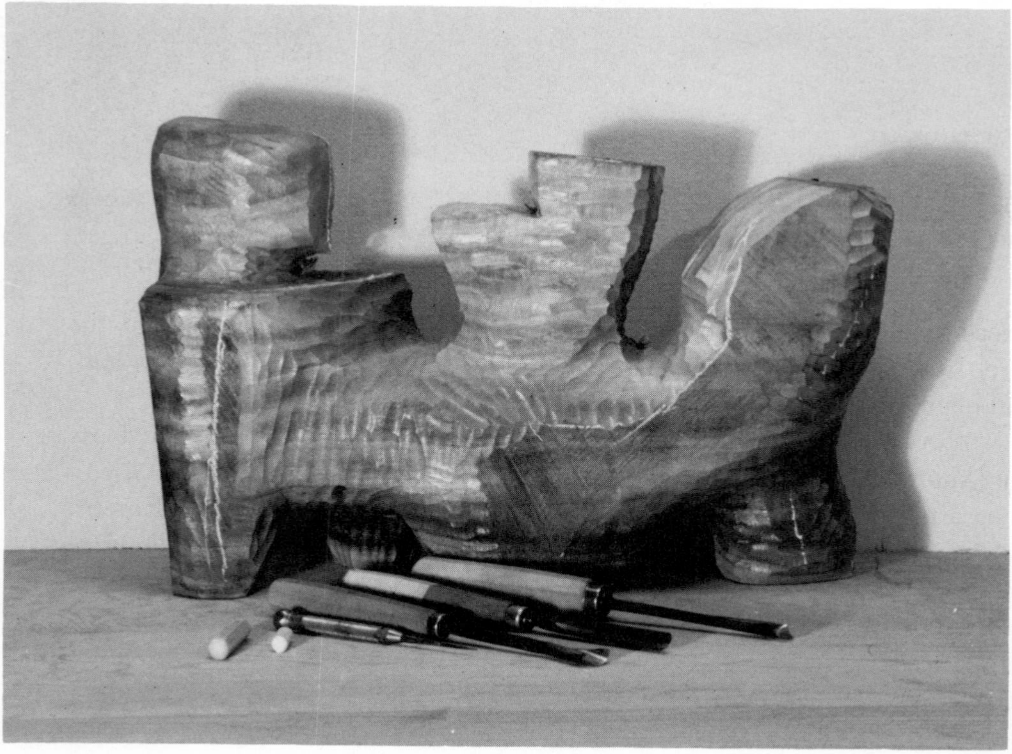

ABOVE LEFT. Fig. 52. I was still having trouble at this point in placing the child properly. Fortunately enough wood has been allowed on all sides to keep the design relatively uncommitted. The design that appeared to work on paper only became obviously wrong when it was applied to the wood. This often happens. These pictures include the tools that have been used thus far in the execution of the piece.

BELOW LEFT. Fig. 53. Now that the baby is placed, we can spend some time developing the shape of the mother. Notice how the chalk is used freely to sketch in guidelines from time to time. The scriber, next to the chalk, is handy for investigating little holes to find out if they are going to become big ones.

BELOW. Fig. 54. The design is committed enough to allow a place for the holding base to be fastened. This is an unusually late time to attach a holder, the delay caused by the tentative nature of the new design. The Surform rasp on the workbench is a very helpful tool.

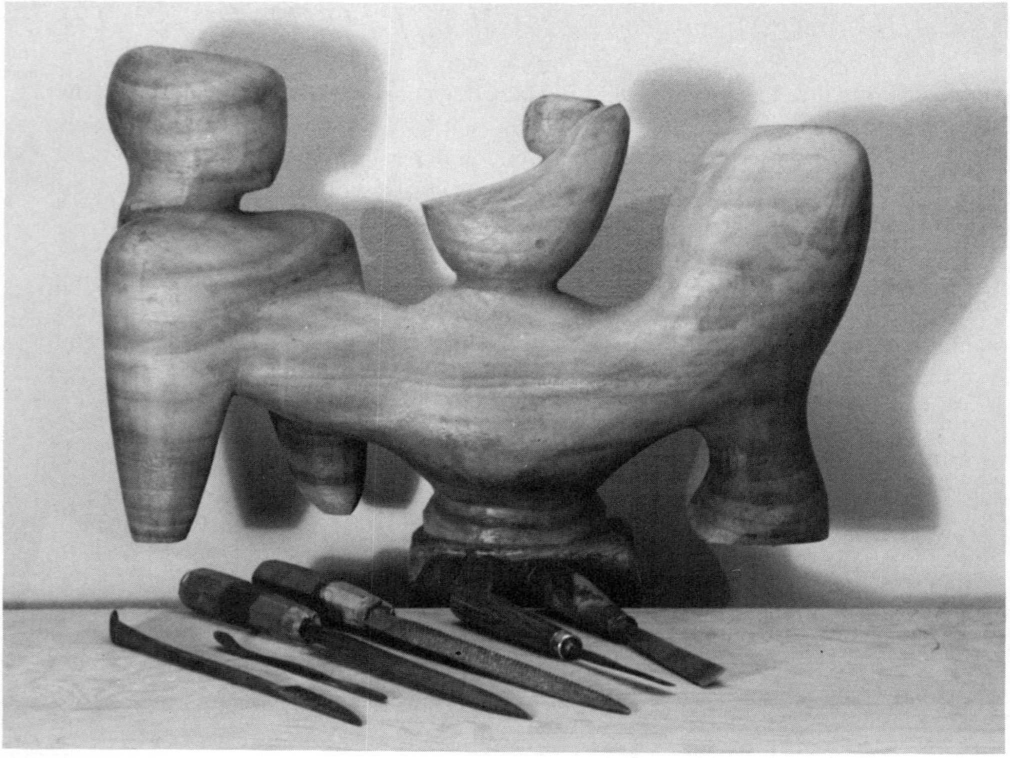

I had prepared my block of wood in such a way that I was still relatively uncommitted. Now that I had adopted an idea it was time to develop it. I developed it in the wood, cutting in such a way that I could modify my design in a number of directions if necessary. This was fortunate, because I was satisfied with the position of the mother, but the child was still giving me trouble. I didn't like him standing up, so I put him down. I drew some more sketches and studied them. Finally I felt that the design had arrived and I began working it into the wood (Fig. 52), leaving each mass bigger than necessary, just in case.

The figure progressed satisfactorily. Once the wood was prepared and the design was shaken down it was a relatively straightforward matter to unwrap the major forms, the minor forms, and eventually the decorative forms.

Another unusual feature of this piece was the amount of time that I worked with it held in my lap. I consciously delayed putting it on a holder since the design was new and untried. It is safer to keep a piece off the holding block until the design is far enough along the ensure screw-holes not marring the finished product. Working without a holding device required great caution to avoid a tragedy, either to the piece or to me. This slowed progress considerably.

I was pleased enough with this idea to try it again later with more success. The struggle to meld an abstract design with a standard theme is a challenge that will never grow old for any artist.

EARTH MOTHER 2

A good example of the importance of anatomy being applied to decidedly abstract work is seen in "Earth Mother 2." She is a theme of basic

ABOVE LEFT. Fig. 55. The figures are just about completed. Notice how the grain is beginning to come out. The two little riffle rasps in the foreground are handy for hard-to-reach places, but they do not take the place of the larger standard rasp and file behind them; they merely speed the completion of the same task.

BELOW LEFT. Fig. 56. Mother and Child (or The Cradle), Monkeypod, 13". Monkeypod finishes with a beautiful luster. The small riffle rasps in the middle cleaned up the last of the tool marks. They were followed by the two scrapers to their left, and then by the three grades of abrasive strips. The fine pad of steel wool on the right finished the job.

Fig. 57. Earth Mother is barely disguised in this rhythmic chunk of Curly Robusta. Most of the flaws are gone. The (?) is a reminder to me that there may be a problem lurking there, but I don't want to remove the wood until the design is well implanted into the wood. There is a chance that it will be perfectly sound.

Fig. 58. We are looking from the head down the body. The interesting concave curve is not too obvious in the other figures. With very few symbolic clues and from an odd angle it is even now apparent that a human figure is beginning to emerge from the wood.

life. She is primordial form. Many would think this piece is a modernistic glob, but there is a lot of anatomy in it despite its abstraction. It is pregnant, fertile and full in the pelvic mass. The protrusions are female and fecund, of that there is no doubt. Formless as it may appear, the anatomy is there. If a line were dropped from the pit of the throat—and even that obscure area's placement is fairly obvious—it would fall directly over the ankle. Anatomy lives, even in a bulbous Earth Mother.

I tried two Earth Mothers in a row. They are of the same wood and possess similar design, and yet they are different. They are excellent examples of the forces of emotion (or aesthetics, if you wish) versus reason (or artistic intellect, if you wish). The first one (Fig. 11) is rawer. It is subtle and apparently unformed, but it imparts a definite personality of its own: a unique feel. The second, the one shown in stages here (Figs. 57 through 61), is a cogent attempt to improve upon the first. Intellect was applied to develop the theme. The mass became more directional. The vertical motion was accentuated. A disparity in size between the upper and lower masses was lessened. The head became four-faced with four eyes rather than two. All of these changes were consciously made to improve the initial concept.

I do not know which one is better, but I have an opinion. I never really *know* what is best—even what I know is just opinion—but I never shrink from making value judgments. You must to maintain your integrity as an artist. To blindly turn one piece out after another without telling yourself whether you are doing better or worse than before is absurd.

My opinion is that probably the first one is better, primarily because it is a more emotional piece. I have long felt that sculptors err when they slight emotion in favor of intellect. I will not defend this statement to my death, but in the small hours of the morning you will probably find that I decidedly lean toward it.

By the way, I made the point earlier that the subject should be one with which the artist is familiar. This obviously is not an absolute truth, as I have never seen an Earth Mother in my life. I have studied and read about Earth Mothers, however, and I do know what I feel about one. This strong feeling and thought about a subject is the requirement for honesty, not personal friendships.

DANCER

As always, it is important to relieve the wood of its flaws before the design is worked into it. Try to hold the design in abeyance until the material is ready. I had hopes that this particular piece of wood (Fig. 62) was going to become a dancer, but that was the extent of my pre-impressions. I was even prepared to abandon that one.

Fig. 59. The major forms are almost completed. Comparing this figure with Fig. 11 shows how small changes in major forms force great changes in over-all design.

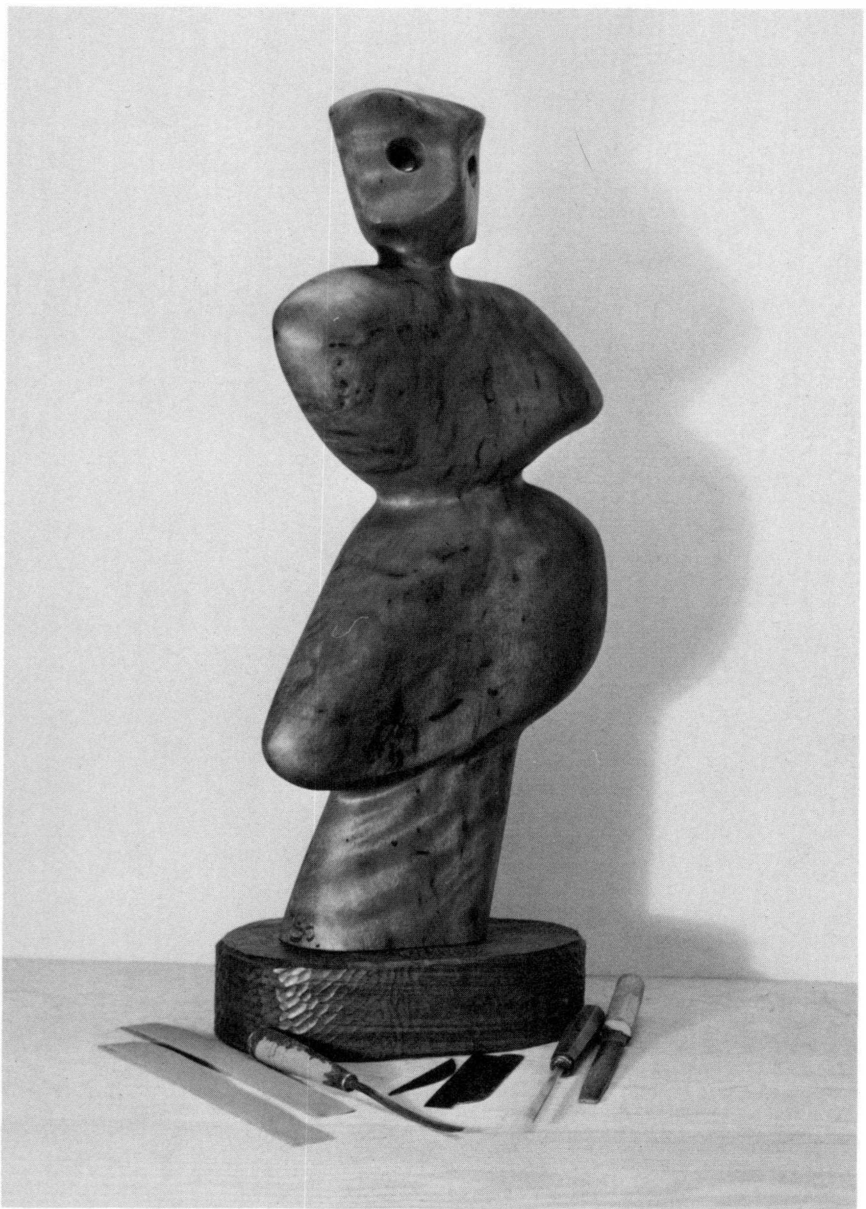

Fig. 60. Almost done. The little metal scrapers at the base of the piece are very helpful in drawing out that glorious grain.

Fig. 61. Earth Mother 2, Curly Robusta, 30". This is the other side of the last figure. Compare this design with that of Fig. 11. Which one do you prefer? Design possibilities are infinite, and the methods of executing them are infinite, also.

Fig. 62. The beginning of the Dancer was this handsome but flawed chunk of rosewood. I have marked all the bad areas with chalk. That crack on the end could be a problem if it goes in too deeply.

A long thin crack ran down the length of the wood, but I chose not to clean it out. I left it because I thought that it would probably not get in the way of my design, but the required removal of wood around it might. It was a gamble. Most of the remaining flaws were cleaned out, and those that were left were probed enough to let me know what I was going to be able to do. One end appeared questionable because of excessive cracking. The bandsaw was helpful here as I used it to slice off two-inch widths from the end. I would then explore the remaining crack with a scriber to try to discern its depth. I did this about five times before I was satisfied that the flaw was bottoming out. All that sawing would have been a chore by hand.

The pictures (Figs. 63 through 68) show the development of the piece. A number of sculptural problems that we have mentioned in previous chapters were overcome in our Dancer. Let's look at a few.

Fig. 63. The indentations at this point are primarily due to removed flaws and not preplanned design. This graphically illustrates the folly of advancing plans too far before the intended wood has been cleaned up. That little upturned point on the left will relieve the base problem later on, but it is obvious here that it was not a human invention; it had to be dealt with, hopefully to the benefit of the piece.

This also depicts the holding block very clearly. It has been screwed onto the rosewood inside. Then it was in turn fastened to the power arm plate with those four large lag-bolts.

Fig. 64. The design is progressing nicely. Those chalked-in guidelines are very helpful in keeping everything in line. Notice how quickly the rosewood has begun to take on the appearance of a dancer.

Great River Regional Library
St. Cloud Public Library
08/18/15 12:29PM
(320) 650-2500
www.griver.org

Checkout

22020009265374

The craft and creation of wood sculptur
32020020763330 Due: Tue, 09/08/15

Decorative woodcarving : the complete c
32020012286928 Due: Tue, 09/08/15

Carving masks : tribal, ethnic & folk p
32020009012030 Due: Tue, 09/08/15

Items: 3
Balance Due $ 0.00

Great River Regional Library
St. Cloud Public Library
08/18/15 12:29PM
(320) 650-2500
www.griver.org

Checkout

22020009265374

The craft and creation of wood sculptur
32020020763330 Due: Tue, 09/08/15

Decorative woodcarving : the complete c
32020012286928 Due: Tue, 09/08/15

Carving masks : tribal, ethnic & folk p
32020009012030 Due: Tue, 09/08/15

Items: 3
Balance Due $ 0.00

Fig. 65. This is the other side a little bit later. The design seems to be working and an upward lift has somehow been generated. This is what we had hoped for. Notice how far in we went at the base. If the holding screws were not grouped at the center we might have had a problem here. The locations of these screws were very much in mind when the wood in that area was removed.

Fig. 66. The forms are completed and ready for texturing, except for the question about the upraised hand. The wire brushes are most helpful in keeping the rasps, files and riffles clean in the process of working.

Fig. 67. The Dancer, Rosewood, 21″ There is a lot of texturing on this piece, but it helps to establish the design of a folkloric dancer. The head was kept smooth for contrast. The base problem and staticism do not seem to hamper this particular piece.

Fig. 68. Dancer from the other side. Although frontality is avoided, it was not done by duplicating the other side. Note that the troublesome upraised hand has been reduced in size.

Base: The 19th Century Romantics had a base problem. Their heroic horse and rider invariably perched on a huge pedestal that engulfed them. More recent sculptors have attacked this problem with some success. Sculpture has to stand on something, of that there is no argument. It is the relationship between this support and the art work that poses the problem. The best support is thin air, but this is difficult to accomplish. We need a base, but what will it be? You must always ask yourself if the base is encumbering the piece. The problem is substantially resolved in the Dancer, not perfectly, but as well as can be done without resorting to trickery.

Frontality: Dancer is three-dimensional. The viewer wants to go around her, and as he goes there is usually something new to see. She has a new silhouette from every angle. The heroic 19th century statue was not as rewarding. A trip around it inevitably led you to the horse's rear end, and all too often it wasn't even a very good horse's rear end.

Staticism: Our Dancer has movement. She does not stand at attention—immobile. Her head is turned a bit, which helps. One arm is a bit different from the other. She is quite abstract, but enough representative clues have been built in so that most people will allow this piece of wood to pass as a dancer. The rhythmic movement helps to achieve this illusion.

Decorative Forms: The head was left untextured to separate it from the body. Contrast is usually interesting, and a smooth surface gives adjoining textured surfaces more character. There is a lot of texturing in this piece. A piece can be butchered by texturing if it is not accompanied by abundant quantities of taste and craftsmanship. It is tedious work, so once you have made your decision to texture you had better prepare to spend some close and careful hours on it. The carving is slow and often boring, but the effect is worth it if the execution has been precise.

SUMMARY

It is obvious, I hope, that doing a full figure is no different in approach and technique from doing a head. Clean the wood, keep the design tentative and work three-dimensionally. Try one now and good luck to you. I recommend that you keep your wood and your design simple and of a moderate size. You can become more grandiose and more experimental later on. Mark the completed piece in your log book and accept my congratulations.

EIGHT

THE ROLES OF A SCULPTOR

A SCULPTOR finds himself filling several roles while he practices the art of sculpturing. First, of course, he is a student. Later on he may become a teacher. As a working sculptor he will wrestle with the intricacies of both the creative process and the business world. Throughout this entire period he will be benefited by some of the blessings of the craft. From student to beneficiary or businessman to creator is quite a span. It might help to look at some of the peculiarities of these categories separately.

STUDENT

The beginner should determine fairly soon whether he enjoys using his hands or not. I once had a good friend who was enrolled in dental school and was interested in the arts. He professed an interest in sculpture and took a few lessons from me. He was terrible. It was apparent that he hated working with his hands. Shortly thereafter he switched from dentistry to eventually become an excellent CPA. He still had an active interest in art, but not as a practitioner. It was fortunate that he could be honest enough with himself to realize that he did not like manual work. It is a chore to do what you don't want to do. Since the student does not rely on his craft for his livelihood, if he doesn't like it he simply won't do it. This is the student's first checkpoint. If it's a drag, drop it.

The next bottleneck for the new student is the famous I'm-going-to-do-a-masterpiece syndrome. Unfortunately he doesn't know enough yet to do a masterpiece. He has got to do a lot of pieces first and learn from his mistakes, of which there will be plenty. He must make his mistakes and get on with it.

TEACHER

Good wood sculpture teachers are scarce. In the thirties there was a handful of direct carvers, each having his own small group of students who slowly drifted away from the medium. World War II spawned the great impetus in welding and other metalworking that drew most everyone away from wood, followed by interest in newer materials, such as plastics. This has resulted in a real shortage of experienced direct carving teachers. For this reason wood sculpture has become something of a lost art. It takes time to become good at it, and that is not currently fashionable. There is quite a technical process to be learned, and this technical process is what has become, quite literally, almost lost. The field needs knowledgeable teachers.

The worst thing about teaching direct carving is the time element. I don't resent it as a teacher, but the student must. In painting it is easy to skip from one process to the next. This does not imply that painting is an easier medium than direct carving, but that it is a more flexible medium to teach. A student sculptor cannot flip to a new practice page and start on the next drawing step. He must laboriously, and usually ineptly, work his way down through the wood to the next level of instruction. This is a real problem in teaching wood sculpture. A class environment should attempt to arrange these catch-up stages between formal sessions so that valuable instruction time is not used up with redundant chipping. Sculpturing technique is like any other: it demands practice to achieve proficiency. A good card shark spends hours in daily practice to master his technique. Doesn't sculpturing demand at least as much devotion and diligence? It takes time to learn to use the tools of direct carving, and the best place to do it is away from the classroom.

All of you who have tried it know that teaching anything is difficult. Art, and particularly sculpturing, surely must lead the list. It is important that each student struggle through his own mistakes to uncover his own solutions. If you are his teacher and do it all for him, why not take his fee and give him a piece of your sculpture in return. It would be much more efficient and the results would be the same. Make the student sweat. It is the only path to real learning.

CREATOR

Glorious fiery inspiration is a myth. Some men become struck by a flash of an idea and jot it down and copy it in wood. That is not creating. That is mimicry. Creativity does not come easily. Many students who have worked around me think that I never experience difficulty because I always seem to be forging ahead. The truth is that I try not to let difficulties stop me in my tracks. The artist's muscle needs steady manipulation for it to function properly.

Artists worry about their wellspring drying up. Many people dry themselves up by overcriticizing their own ideas. It is better to find out if your idea is bad by applying it to wood and seeing for yourself. Do not bind yourself up with your own hypercriticism.

Sometimes ideas do come easier and faster than usual. Jot them down on paper while they are fresh. Don't ignore them just because it isn't the right time of day to think creatively. Then go back at a quieter moment and sift through these jottings. Improve on them if you can, and proceed. If you can control it, this is the best of two worlds. You are taking advantage of the occasional rush of creativity without becoming a slave to its whims.

BUSINESSMAN

A successful sculptor is a good businessman as well as a good artist. A few items need tending to no matter how ethereal your artistic outlook may be.

Pricing: There are two rules about pricing. The first is difficult for the idealistic young artist to accept. That is that there is no correlation between the amount of work invested in creating a piece and its price. The customer does not want to pay more for a piece just because you had difficulty producing it. I recently had trouble finishing a piece and it took about twice as long as it should have. The piece following seemed to flow from the chisel and I did it in half the usual time. Both of the finished products are similar in artistic value, in my opinion. I cannot set the price of the more difficult piece four times higher than the other or the customer is going to lose faith in my pricing scheme. Prices based on work expended are not convincing to the art customer. It seems more sensible to him, no matter how much we may privately deplore the fact, to set prices based on the mass of material in the piece. A big piece costs more than a little piece. We may swallow hard at times when we set our prices this way, but it does make more sense to the buyer.

The second rule is not quite so hard to comprehend, although it is constantly ignored by too many artists. A woman in New York taught me long ago the secret of price ranges. If you are not selling, your prices are too high; if you are selling and can't keep up with the demand, your prices are too low. It is the last bastion of free enterprise's law of supply and demand. The death of many artists has been caused by letting their products pile up around them. It is death by constipation. It is better to give the things away, burn them or bury them, but get them away from you. I try to stay somewhat underpriced in order to save myself from this unsavory artistic death.

Dealers: I have enjoyed good relationships with a number of dealers, but one must always be wary of those few dealers who are not properly concerned about the artist. They prey on many artists in the good but not great category. The artist deals exclusively with one gallery, and eventually the gallery will bend with the currents of contemporary taste and say, "Thanks, but we don't want any more." That is the end of that. The artist is never seen or heard from again.

Many more successful artists suffer from another common malady: they can't say no. Their dealers badger them to turn out more work and never mind the quality. They aren't strong enough to constantly turn this down, and I am not sure who would be. This is the reason for the unevenness in the quality of their later work. Picasso suffers from this problem. If he had an excrement on the sidewalk and cast it he would get $10,000 for it. The name is there and the dealer is beckoning, so it becomes cast and sold. This is a danger for the successful artist, a danger that I hope you enjoy.

Taxes: If you continue in your craft you will eventually begin to sell your work rather than give it away. I urge you to keep detailed records of these sales and to report them on your income tax return. Many people don't. They feel that sculpturing is an avocation for them and that what little money they make from it is gravy to be enjoyed. Besides, they don't make enough in this way to matter. This may be true at first, but it is surprising how these sales can build into sizable profits. It is best to handle these in a businesslike fashion and not worry about it. One fine benefit from reporting sales is that you can deduct costs related to sculpturing. As we saw in an earlier chapter, tools and material can become quite costly. Writing them off on your tax return eases the pain considerably.

BENEFICIARY

We gain much from the arts, particularly when we actively practice them. A few of these assets bear mentioning.

Tactility: I have learned to see with my hands. This first came to my attention during an outdoor public demonstration by several painters and sculptors under lights. Suddenly the lights went out. The only light came from distant streetlights. It was dark and everyone stopped working except me. I found to my amazement that I could continue because I had developed a habit of constantly running my hand over the piece to feel its condition rather than to see it. Since then I don't trust my eye to see if a form is true. I run my hand over it instead. This extreme sensitivity of hands was a revelation to me and it has added a dimension to the enjoyment of living. I often display little signs at my shows that read, "PLEASE TOUCH." I want my audience to discover this tactile pleasure, too.

Brain-freedom: One of the most desirable aspects of this craft is the way that it lets you think while you are practicing it. This is a blessing that my writer friends and musician friends don't have. We do. It is pleasant to be able to work on a piece and listen attentively to conversation or music, or to think unrelated thoughts.

Awareness: This is an amorphous word, but it seems evident that exposure to the arts, particularly in practice, develops a heightened sense of the drama of life as it swirls about one. Compassion and a respect for life will emerge from your work as surely as do the wood chips falling to the floor. This might seem a strange point to make in a book of this sort, but it is a condition so basic and so fulfilling that it deserves to be spelled out for all to contemplate. Enjoy it.

NINE

EXTENDING THE ART

THE only way to truly know a subject is to extend it to its limits. First learn your craft, then try to expand your knowledge, ability and personal satisfaction with it. This is best done in two ways: extending the creative process and extending the material.

EXTENDING THE CREATIVE PROCESS

This has already been discussed in detail. The creative process is stretched by not committing ourselves too soon and by delaying that time when we are merely copying our mind's preset ideas. Commitment can be forestalled at times other than execution also. We can stay flexible during the design period by refusing to accept any specific drawing or sketch as final. Forcing the mind to continually look for a new approach to a problem is an extension of creative time. Even when you think you have a good sketch, do a few more. You will find this stretching of the imagination to be most enriching. Just remember that when you pick up a piece of wood there are a million different designs you could impart into that wood, and a million different ways that you could impart them, and I mean literally millions. Think lively and be copious with your ideas.

Fig. 69. The Vicissitudes of Man, Peruvian Mahogany, 45″. The two end pieces swing back and forth on brass rod hinges. Constructing the rounded surfaces surrounding the hinges was very difficult, but the overall effect was successful. This hinging idea was not just a stunt, but instead an attempt to add depth to the theme by presenting it in triptych fashion.

EXTENDING THE MATERIAL

There are many ways to extend the uses of wood. Some people have done work with laminations, such as plywood. The results haven't been too successful, but that doesn't mean they will continue to be unsuccessful. There have also been abortive attempts to use wood as if it were a different material, but I choose not to dwell upon this type of hypocrisy. Two better extensions of wood are through using color and making assemblies.

COLOR

Polychrome is something that sculptors have always experimented with, again with little success. If you try this technique you will want to use acrylic paint. Oil paint never completely dries. Acrylic does. It will dry hard in one day, after which you can sand it or work it like any wood surface. It finishes glossy or non-glossy, as you wish, and it is compatible with Watco oil and other finishes. Acrylics flow over textured areas very well, neither skipping deep grooves nor filling them up. Think before you apply the paint, however, as it will be impossible to remove it from the grooves of textured areas without removing the texture, also.

ASSEMBLIES OF SECTIONS

Combining different parts into one unified piece of sculpture is a prime example of material extension. This is not a common approach, but it often works quite well in achieving an effect beyond the reach of a single block of wood.

"The Vicissitudes of Man" (Fig. 69) is an attempt to extend wood through hinging it in triptych fashion. The hinges are arranged so that the piece appears to be a unified mass when at rest. The combination of three pieces of wood adds a dimension that a single piece could not give. The material has been extended without lying about it.

"The Family Unit" (Fig. 70) has wooden pegs holding it together. There are eight separate pieces, all of walnut. This treatment supports the theme in a physical manner that is denied to a single mass.

MULTI-SCULPTURAL ASSEMBLIES

A real challenge to the artist is to extend the uses of wood by combining several small but individual pieces into a unified assembly. This work is advanced. It is technically difficult to make small pieces, and even more difficult to put them together into a meaningful unit. A small piece is defined here as being less than a foot high and an inch or two in width, so it is obvious the designs will be limited and the technique critical.

Wood Selection: Most of the raw material will be scrap wood (Fig. 71). It is wasteful to cut up logs for this sort of project so we will use up the splinters instead. They are usually too small to be used for any-

Fig. 70. Family Unit, Walnut, 37″. Fabricating several different sections into one unit adds to the theme of the piece.

Fig. 71. This is the sort of source material we need to make working on assemblies worth the effort. Many varieties of wood in many shapes promise to offer interesting combinations.

thing else. The power saw is helpful in cleaning up the many sides of these wood fragments. Remember, there is no virtue in refraining from power tools, as long as they are used carefully and cautiously.

Design: We want to work wildly and experimentally with these little pieces. We are trying to develop new facets in our vocabulary such as new forms and new uses of space. Out of this entire batch of individual pieces there may come one new idea that can be used in future work.

Fig. 72. After using the power saw to clean up our stock-pile it looks much better. Most of these pieces are too small to be used for a more standard sculptural work, and it is a pleasure to be able to use them for something other than starting fires. This is a picture of the most expensive kindling in America.

Lignum vitae, for example, is a very hard wood. I would like to see if this hardness can be displayed by leaving obvious chisel marks on the surface. Maybe it won't work, but at least I will have tried it and will have learned without jeopardizing a larger piece of this expensive wood and a larger portion of my time and energy.

It is important that you divide your soul in two when producing these multi-sculptural assemblies. Design each individual piece separately, with no thought whatsoever of any assembly scheme. This will stretch your imagination and creativity. When you have completed them you can stretch your imagination again by trying to put them together. This is not easy. This is advanced sculpturing, and these assemblies can be most exasperating.

I enjoy with vicious glee being the designer of these little units, chortling over the agony that the poor final assembler (me) is going to experience in trying to put them together into a meaningful pattern. An artificial problem is created, and the struggle to solve it often results in a work that is successful in extending the art.

These little sculptures of different design and different wood challenge my skill. Why not plan the assembly first and then prepare the specific pieces? Aside from missing the mind-expanding task of devising a solution, this approach would also result in a contrived solution. The creative process would have been lobotomized from the project and nothing of value would have been gained. These small pieces are approached just as the bigger pieces are. The only difference is that you will need extra pencils and paper to sketch all your experimental ideas, and you will probably be trying to strive for a magical quality and a chance to try out new ideas.

You will need to know the characteristics of the various woods that you select. Rosewood, for example, is not brittle and can take any kind of lateral movement. Therefore a rosewood design can be attenuated. Teak, on the other hand, splits easily and so it should be treated more as a solid mass. Zebrawood doesn't split and can be used in a delicate fashion. This is the sort of thing you should know to best utilize the varieties of wood you will be employing.

Holding Devices: No matter how small the work, it still has to be held in place or it will bounce around with the chisel and you will lose control. Fig. 73 shows how most of these pieces have an extended base on them which will be used to mount onto a holding device. Eventually

Fig. 73. Several individual pieces have been started. Refer to page 153 for the alphabetical key. Notice the notched bases in the foreground and how the other woods are mounted on standard holding devices in the background. A previous attempt at multi-sculptural assemblies appears in the middle to give you an idea of what we are up to.

these bases will be chiseled off and thrown away. Holding devices are a problem with these small pieces because there is so little wood available on which to make a purchase. Everything has to be scaled down. Use small wood screws instead of the larger ones we used before. It is often advisable to attach a plate to the extra base piece we have provided, and then to attach that plate to a vise. Lag screws would crack out such a small piece, so you need to make tiny grabs with about eight screws to hold it firmly. The grain will be flowing across the base of some of these small pieces, so be sure to scatter the screws around the base so the grain lines won't be wedged open.

Most of these small woods I am using are hard woods. When drilling screw holes in hard wood it is important that they are not too small or the screw will become a wedge and the material will crack. The hole diameter should almost be the diameter of the threads, and its depth should be that of the screw. Test out the hole on a piece of scrap wood first. These may seem like extra steps, but these few minutes will save you hours of heartache. Turn the screws all the way down. If one strips, use a slightly longer screw. Two or three screws will hold, but if the wood starts to wobble you are in trouble. I have been miserly with screws before, only to have to stop and try to put in some more, only to crack the wood. Naturally we won't need to level the base of these small pieces because the base won't be there when we are finished.

Shaping: Remember, each of these is to be treated like a big piece, so don't commit yourself. We will go through exactly the same steps with these as we would with a big piece. We still have to clean the wood, develop the major forms, then the minor, and finally the decorative. These are valid sculptural objects, designed and shaped in exactly the same manner as larger pieces.

There are only two differences: the margin for uncommitment is smaller; and doing these assemblies is messy, confusing and persnickety. Shifting gears from working normally to making assemblies is a shock, because you are using so many different grain colors, so many different woods, all in so many different combinations, with accompanying scale problems, texture problems and construction problems. Eventually you have to stop just before complete insanity sets in. Your workshop is in total turmoil and so is your head, but that is part of the whole idea: to stretch your imagination and your technique.

I primarily use exotic woods in assemblies because of the dramatic

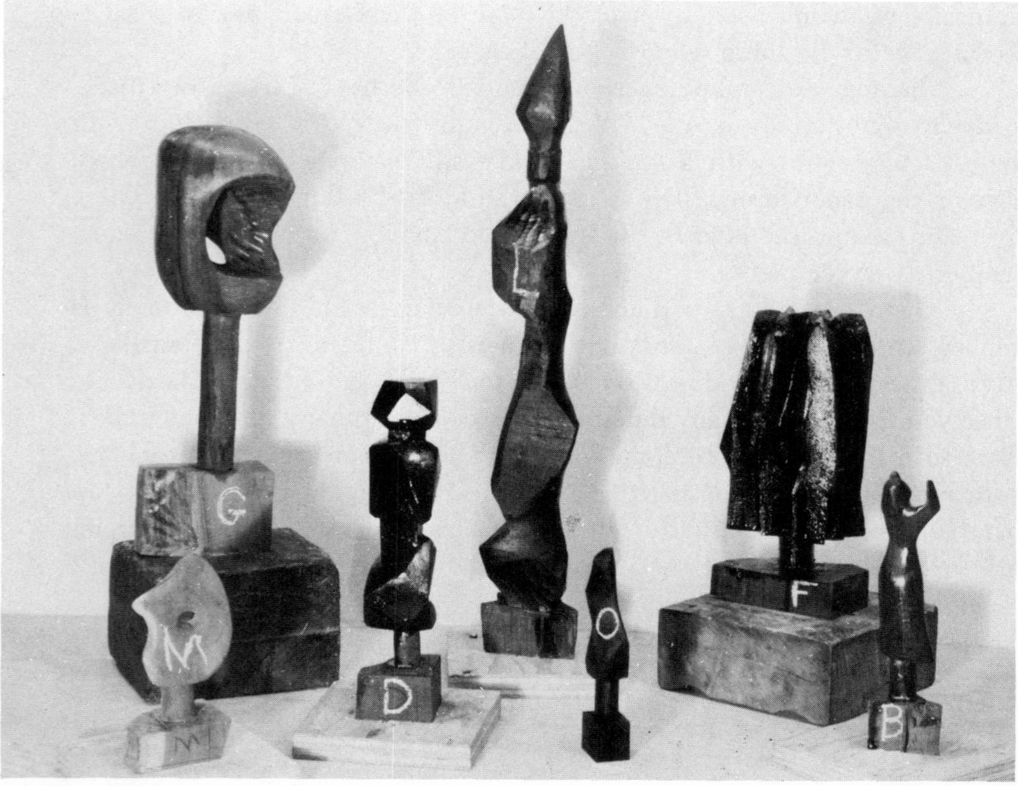

character of the grain and because of their magical, jewel-like quality. The woods used in this group are identified in the pictures by the following letter codes:

A	Lignum vitae	12 inches
B	Snakewood	8
C	Zebrawood	6½
D	Ebony	10
E	Teak	12
F	Ebony	10
G	Koa	13½
H	Ebony	13½
J	Rosewood	20
K	Monkeypod	10½
L	Rosewood	20
M	Milo	6
N	Milo	12
O	Ebony	3½
P	Rosewood	20
R	Myrtlewood burl	16
S	Milo	22
T	Mahogany	14
U	Koa	16
W	Vermillion	22
X	Vermillion	5

This particular batch of individual pieces took longer for me to prepare than I had planned. I am making each piece more involved than the one before in an attempt to extend myself and to extend my material. It is also slower making pieces for many multiple assemblies at once. I recommend you do not do this at first. Make enough for one and quit. As we

ABOVE LEFT. Fig. 74. The individual pieces have been brought further along at this point. It is surprising how many different design ideas can be gleaned from these small pieces of wood.

BELOW LEFT. Fig. 75. Here is another group of individual pieces that have progressed into an advanced stage. It is tempting to imagine combinations of these little sculptures, but to be successful one must put off this activity until the first job of creating the individual sculptures is completely finished.

Fig. 76. Notice how the sculptural piece (D) has been removed from its base (D). Now that it is completed the base can be discarded. A small peg-like structure is left on the piece to allow it to fit into some other wood. The plumb-bob is helpful in making these little pieces vertical. The board with the multi-sized holes in it is a very handy device that allows me to get the bases concentric and to try out various combinations of sculptures.

grow older we become more masochistic and do these terrible things to ourselves.

Transition: There comes a point where you must stop creating individual pieces and must start to think about putting them together. You must literally change hats. This is difficult, because you will find yourself actively chastising the creative inventiveness which so recently made you proud.

I began with the idea of creating very difficult problems with absolutely no concern about how these problems were to be resolved. I had

Fig. 77. I had to cheat a little to get my first assembly going by lopping a piece of myrtlewood burl off a larger chunk. The lopping was expensive, as it uncovered those two bullets in the foreground. It is fascinating how many of these bullets are found in wood. I don't mind the Civil War lead ones, but the modern steel-jacketed ones invariably ruin a tool. See how snooty L, J and P are. They realize they have caused me a lot of trouble, and they are right.

succeeded gloriously. An artist should be somewhat schizophrenic: partly a creator and partly a craftsman. One entity should never worry about the other. The craftsman should have nothing to say about the design he is to carry out. Whether it is easy or hard to execute should not matter. I am sure that I have never changed a design to make it easier for me to execute, but of course I am not sure whether I have been kidding myself or not. If we fret about whether a new design can be accomplished, it probably never will be.

Curse yourself all you want. If you have been honest you will now have some wildly designed pieces to put together somehow, and perhaps you will produce an assembly that has validity and freshness. Cherish this hope while you curse.

Assembling: The next day wasn't quite as black, and I proceeded with all deliberate speed.

"Enchanted Landscape" (Fig. 79): I started by selecting some vertical figures. I had made similar figures before, but had always flattened one side so that they would fit together and would mount at a certain height. This time I purposely designed them without flat sides, so now the problem was how to mount them. I finally decided on an enchanted landscape, out of Tolkien's Middle Earth, perhaps. This would unify the figures. It was a good idea but hard to construct. It is terribly difficult to get irregular shapes to fit together. At times like this you wish you had a little man sitting in the tight spots who could tell you exactly where one piece was high and rubbing against the other. We don't have a little man so we will use a piece of chalk instead. Rub the chalk on the mounting surface of one piece and insert it carefully into the other. Then remove it and examine it. Where the chalk is rubbed off is a high spot and must be removed, but not too much at once. Proceed cautiously. This is an old machinist's trick, by the way, but it works just fine for us. It is important that these pieces fit snugly together, and our chalk will ensure that.

"The Return of the God to the Island" (Fig. 80): I have become intrigued in my reading by the way the Pacific islanders always seem to be hauling their gods back and forth across the water. It was as if the primary inter-island commerce was gods' transportation. This notion that I had stored away was probably triggered by the undulating chip form (S) which suggested a boat to me. It is milo, which comes from Hawaii, and is hard to find. All of these things helped to suggest the theme.

Fig. 78. The pieces have been removed from their bases. At this point I was struggling to get them to fit snugly into the center section (R).

"Europa and the Bull" (Fig. 81): I have always wanted to do one of these. You can follow the progress of the bull's head in Figs. 73 and 74. His body is first seen in Fig. 78. As in larger pieces, apply Watco oil or any other finish when you think you are done. After it dries any marring tool marks will come to light. Carefully clean these and refinish.

ABOVE LEFT. Fig. 79. The Enchanted Landscape, Myrtlewood Burl and Rosewood, 19". Done! Without the chalk trick these things would never have gone together.

BELOW LEFT. Fig. 80. Return of the Gods to the Island, Ebony and Milo, 10". My little islander god looks as if he were an inveterate surfer.

ABOVE. Fig. 81. Europa and the Bull, Milo, Zebrawood and Peruvian Mahogany, 13". I think you can pick out the Bull's head. I'll leave the rest of the symbolism to your own tastes. Perhaps you have seen better presentations of this theme, but remember that my ground rules were a little rough. I think the piece works.

Fig. 82. The Oracle, Koa, Snakewood, Milo, Monkeypod, 12″. Notice how the touches of texturing in the base tend to pull the group together.

"The Oracle" (Fig. 82): This is a good example of a design in which I knew exactly what I was doing but it might not be too obvious to the viewer. He will associate the title with the piece and be satisfied, but I actually had a further nuance in mind.

Superstitions and myths, such as oracles, endure only when they seem to function in our lives. Oracles fulfill a need. The King, for example, or any other dupe of similar stature, frets about a problem. His evil advisor says, "Say, you better go ask the Oracle." Then the advisor runs out and hides behind the oracle and tells the king whatever he wants the king to hear. That is the role of the third piece in this assembly: the evil advisor.

Take your choice about the symbols. The piece should have a quality of magic and it should hold together aesthetically. That is the prerequisite. The rest of it is my conceit. If you like my idea, fine. If you see something else, that's all right, too. The point I want to make is that I had a definite

Fig. 83. Phantasm, Vermillion, Ebony, Koa, Lignum Vitae, Teak, 17". The four (X)'s act as leg supports. This is a helpful reminder that all individual pieces do not end up with glorious roles in the final assembly.

Fig. 84. Magic Return of the Gods, mixed woods, 17". This theme obviously stemmed from the earlier idea about the islander god traveller. This is one of three collages assembled from the remaining individual pieces.

concept in mind when I began, and I followed it through. I knew exactly what I was doing, but I don't require the viewer to know exactly what it is.

"Phantasm" (Fig. 83): This could be considered another variation of the oracle theme, but this is not necessarily the case. What is pertinent is whether the combination of woods and designs resulted in an interesting assembly.

The collage pictured in Figure 84, along with two others, exhausted our inventory of little pieces and scraps. These last assemblies took much longer to complete than they should have. I had already used most of my raw material and so was somewhat constricted for ideas. I was also trying to use all of my individual pieces in these assemblies for purposes of this book. Ordinarily I would set any recalcitrant pieces aside for the next assembly exercise, which I usually do about once a year.

SUMMARY

The benefits gained by constructing multi-sculptural assemblies are obvious. I expanded my creative time by working in isolation on each individual piece, and then by putting them together into valid assemblies. The wood has been extended by combining it with other woods to do things that it could not do alone. I stretched myself by developing new ideas and an open way of working with a minimum loss in time and material.

The negative side is obvious, too. The workroom is in chaos. You hate your own ingenuity. Worst of all, you cannot afford to do this very often. If you are making a living with your sculpture you can't exist on ten cents an hour and that's about what this approach will net you. You should set some time aside for these experiments, though, because it will push your sculptural horizons outward by extending you, your material, and your craft.

If you have not already done so, examine the Appendices for information on wood, tools and books. They may prove helpful to you.

APPENDICES

A Suppliers of Tools
B Suppliers of Wood
C Wood Chart
D Suggested Bibliography

SUPPLIERS OF TOOLS

These few suppliers, listed in alphabetical order, are offered only to help you get started. Their appearance here does not necessarily imply an endorsement. Revised 1981.

1. Alexander's Sculptural Service
   117 East 39th Street
   New York, New York 10016

2. Buck Bros., Inc.
   P. O. Box 192
   Millbury, Massachusetts 01527

3. Albert Constantine
   2050 Eastchester Road
   Bronx, New York 10461

4. Lee Valley Tools, Ltd.
   857 Boyd Ave.
   Ottawa, Ontario, Canada
   K2A 2C9

5. Minnesota Woodworkers
   21801 Industrial Blvd.
   Rogers, Minnesota 55374

6. Sculpture Associates, Ltd., Inc.
   114 East 25th St.
   New York, New York 10010

7. Sculpture House
   38 East 30th St.
   New York, New York 10016

8. Woodcarvers Supply Co.
   3056 Excelsior Blvd.
   Minneapolis, Minnesota 55416

9. Woodcraft Supply Corp.
   313 Montvale Ave.
   Woburn, Massachusetts 01801

APPENDIX B

SUPPLIERS OF WOOD

Between the time of originating this book and the time of preparing a list of wood suppliers most of my commercial suppliers removed themselves from the sculptural supply business. Be thankful that wood is where you find it. A few contacts (revised 1981) are:

1. Albert Constantine
   2050 Eastchester Road
   Bronx, New York 10461

2. Craftsman Hardwood Lumber Co. (domestic)
   13005 S. Western Ave.
   Blue Island, Illinois 60406

3. Lee Valley Tools, Ltd.
   857 Boyd Ave.
   Ottawa, Ontario, Canada K2A 2C9

4. Minnesota Woodworkers
   21801 Industrial Blvd.
   Rogers, Minnesota 55374

5. Sculpture Associates, Ltd., Inc. (foreign, domestic)
   114 East 25th St.
   New York, New York 10010

6. Sculpture House (foreign, domestic)
   38 East 30th St.
   New York, New York 10016

7. Woodcarvers Supply Co.
   3056 Excelsior Blvd.
   Minneapolis, Minnesota 55416

8. Woodcraft Supply Corp.
   313 Montvale Ave.
   Woburn, Massachusetts 01801

APPENDIX C

WOOD CHART—DOMESTIC WOOD

	APPEARANCE			CHARACTERISTICS		AVAILABILITY	
Name	**Basic Color**	**Color Variety**	**Grain Variety**	**Hardness**	**Workability**	**Form**	**Supply**
Apple	Creamy white	Minimum	Fine, close	Hard	Good	2, 3	Good
Birch	Light	Variable	Medium	Med/Hard	Fair	1, 2	Fair
Butternut	Light golden tan	Variable	Variable	Med/Hard	Excellent	2, 3	Poor
Cedar	Red	Variable	Variable	Brittle/Hard	Fair	2, 3	Good
Cherry	Reddish	Minimum	Fine/Close	Hard	Excellent	2, 3	Good
Cypress	Yellow white	Variable	Variable	Soft	Fair	2, 3	Fair
Elm	Light to dark brown	Variable	Variable	Med/Hard	Fair	2, 3	Good
Hedge	Yellow	Variable	Coarse	Hard	Difficult	2, 3	Fair
Linden (Basswood)	Creamy white	Variable	Fine/Close	Soft	Excellent	2	Fair
Maple		Variable	Fine/Close		Fair	2	Fair
Myrtle	Creamy white	Variable	Fine	Hard	Fair	2	Fair
Myrtlewood Burl		Variable	Mixed		Excellent	3	Good
Oak		Variable	Mixed	Hard	Good	2, 3	Good
Pear	Creamy white	Minimum	Close	Med/Hard	Excellent	2	Good
Persimmon	White	Minimum	Close	Hard	Good	2	Fair
Walnut	Brown	Minimum	Medium/Close	Hard	Excellent	1, 2, 3	Good
Wild Cherry	Reddish white	Variable	Close	Hard	Excellent	2	Poor

Because of the wide range of characteristics within each species it is difficult to be precise. Where even a general description would seem misleading we have left it blank.

FORM: 1—Square cut lumber; 2—Small short logs; 3—Free forms (stumps, driftwood, etc.).

WOOD CHART—HAWAIIAN WOOD

	APPEARANCE			CHARACTERISTICS		AVAILABILITY	
Name	Basic Color	Color Variety	Grain Variety	Hardness	Workability	Form	Supply
Breadfruit Ulu	Chartreuse, tan	Faint Banding	Minimum	Med/Soft	Good	1, 2	Fair
Coffee	Creamy white	None	Minimum	Hard	Fair	2, 3	Poor
Hau	Grey-black	Variable	Minimum	Med/Soft	Excellent	2, 3	Poor
Jacaranda	Light golden tan	Light banding	Minimum	Medium	Excellent	1, 2	Fair
Kamani	Medium red	Medium banding	Variable	Med/Hard	Fair	1, 2, 3	Good
Koa	Golden red-brown to black	Distinct banding	Curly, birdseye	Medium	Excellent	1, 3	Excellent
Kou	Grey-black	Variable	Minimum	Med/Soft	Excellent	2, 3	Poor
Kauila	Dark brown	Variable	Minimum	Very Hard	Fair	2, 3	Poor
Mango	Gold, grey-black	Variable	Curly	Medium	Excellent	1, 2, 3	Excellent
Milo	Dark red-brown to black	Variable	Variable	Medium	Excellent	2, 3	Fair
Monkey Pod	White to dark brown	Distinct banding	Variable	Medium	Good	1, 2, 3	Good
Naio	Chartreuse, tan	Light banding	Curly, birdseye	Hard	Good	1, 2, 3	Good
Robusta, Curly	Old rose	Light banding	Curly	Hard	Fair	1, 3	Fair
Sandalwood	Golden tan	Faint Banding	Minimum	Hard	Fair	2, 3	Fair
Yellow Poinciana	Gold to red-brown	Variable	Variable	Med/Hard	Good	1, 2	Poor

Species most commonly used in Hawaii for craft manufacturing are Monkey Pod, Koa, Milo (when available), Mango and Kamani. Kou and dark Hau are also highly esteemed, but supply is difficult. The finest craftwood for all purposes, including sculpturing, is Milo. The other species listed have been used with varying success, volume use restricted by public color preference, difficulty of supply or problems with wood characteristics.

FORM: 1—Square cut lumber; 2—Small short logs; 3—Free forms (stumps, driftwood, etc.).

WOOD CHART—FOREIGN WOOD

	APPEARANCE			CHARACTERISTICS		AVAILABILITY	
Name	Basic Color	Color Variety	Grain Variety	Hardness	Workability	Form	Supply
Amaranth	Red	Minimum	Minimum	Med/Hard	Good	1	Good
Avodire	Light mixed	Variable	Variable	Med/Hard	Good	1, 2	Fair
Beefwood	Purple brown	Minimum	Dense, even	Hard	Difficult	1	Poor
Cocobolo	Reddish brown	Variable	Variable	Hard	Difficult	1, 2	Fair
Ebony	Brown to black	Variable	Dense, close	Hard	Excellent	1, 2	Good
Grenadilla	Black	None	Dense, close	Hard	Excellent	1, 2	Poor
Ipplewood	Rich brown	Variable	Close, fine	Hard	Excellent	2	Poor
Lignum Vitae	White and dark brown	Variable	Dense, close	Hard	Excellent	2	Fair
Mahogany	Reddish	None	Open	Med/Hard	Good	1	Good
Primavera	Rich blond	Variable	Variable	Hard	Good	1, 2	Fair
Rosewood	Rich red-brown	Variable	Variable	Hard	Excellent	1, 2	Fair
Satin	Light yellow	Ornamental	Variable	Medium	Good	1	Poor
Snake	Warm reddish brown	Black spots	Dense	Hard	Good	1, 2	Poor
Teak	Yellow golden brown	Variable	Coarse	Med/Hard	Good	2	Fair
Tulipwood	Red and yellow streaks	Variable	Variable	Hard	Good	2	Poor
Vermillion	Wine red	None	Close	Medium	Good	1	Fair
Zebra	Brown and yellow streaks	Minimum	Coarse	Med/Hard	Good	1	Fair

Because of the wide range of characteristics within each species it is difficult to be precise. Where even a general description would seem misleading we have left it blank.

FORM: 1—Square cut lumber; 2—Small short logs; 3—Free forms (stumps, driftwood, etc.).

APPENDIX D

SUGGESTED BIBLIOGRAPHY

This list is by no means all-inclusive, but it will lead you to a few other books that can in turn send you outward to further references.

GENERAL

1. Donna Z. Meilach, *Contemporary Art with Wood,* Crown, 1968.
2. Jack C. Rich, *The Materials and Methods of Sculpture,* Oxford, 1947.
3. John Rood, *Sculpture in Wood,* Univ. of Minnesota, 1950.
4. William Zorach, *Zorach Explains Sculpture,* American Artists Group, 1947.

ANATOMY

1. George B. Bridgman, *Drawing from Life,* Sterling, 1952.
2. Richard G. Hatton, *Figure Drawing,* Chapman and Hall.
3. Andrew Loomis, *Figure Drawing,* Viking, 1944.

INDEX